PANSIES

PANSIES

POEMS
BY
D. H. LAWRENCE

Fredonia Books
Amsterdam, The Netherlands

Pansies

by
D. H. Lawrence

ISBN: 1-58963-674-0

Copyright © 2002 by Fredonia Books

Reprinted from the 1930 edition

Fredonia Books
Amsterdam, The Netherlands
http://www.fredoniabooks.com

All rights reserved, including the right to reproduce this book, or portions thereof, in any form.

In order to make original editions of historical works available to scholars at an economical price, this facsimile of the original edition of 1930 is reproduced from the best available copy and has been digitally enhanced to improve legibility, but the text remains unaltered to retain historical authenticity.

FOREWORD

These poems are called "PANSIES" because they are rather "PENSÉES" than anything else. Pascal or La Bruyère wrote their "PENSÉES" in prose, but it has always seemed to me that a real thought, a single thought, not an argument, can only exist easily in verse, or in some poetic form. There is a didactic element about prose thoughts which makes them repellent, slightly bullying. "He who hath wife and children hath given hostages to fortune." There is a thought well put; but immediately it irritates by its assertiveness. It applies too direct to actual practical life. If it were put into poetry it wouldn't nag at us so practically. We don't want to be nagged at.

So I should wish these "PANSIES" to be taken as thoughts rather than anything else; casual thoughts that are true while they are true and irrelevant when the mood and circumstance changes. I should like them to be as fleeting as pansies, which wilt so soon, and are so fascinating with their varied faces, while they last. And flowers, to my thinking, are not merely pretty-pretty. They have in their fragrance an earthiness of the humus and the corruptive earth from which they spring. And pansies, in their streaked faces, have a look of many things besides hearts-ease.

Some of the poems are perforce omitted—about a dozen from the bunch. When Scotland Yard seized the MS. in the post, at the order of the Home Secretary, no doubt there was a rush of detectives, postmen, and Home Office clerks and heads, to pick out the most lurid blossoms. They must have been very disappointed. When I now read down the list of the omitted poems, and recall the dozen amusing, not terribly important bits of pansies *which have had to stay out of print for fear a policeman might put his foot on them, I can only grin once more to think of the nanny-goat, nanny-goat in-a-white-petticoat silliness of it all. It is like listening to a Mrs Caudle's curtain lecture in the next house, and wondering whether Mrs Caudle is funnier, or Mr Caudle; or whether they aren't both of them merely stale and tedious.*

Anyhow I offer a bunch of pansies, not a wreath of immortelles. *I don't want everlasting flowers, and I don't want to offer them to anybody else. A flower passes, and that perhaps is the best of it. If we can take it in its transience, its breath, its maybe mephistophelian, maybe palely ophelian face, the look it gives, the gesture of its full bloom, and the way it turns upon us to depart—that was the flower, we have had it, and no* immortelle *can give us anything in comparison. The same with the pansy poems; merely the breath of the moment, and one eternal moment easily contradicting the next eternal moment. Only don't nail the pansy down. You won't keep it any better if you do.*

D. H. LAWRENCE.

BANDOL, *March* 1929.

CONTENTS

	PAGE
Our Day is over	15
Hark in the Dusk!	15
Elephants in the Circus	15
Elephants plodding	16
On the Drum	16
Two Performing Elephants	16
Twilight	17
Cups	17
Bowls	17
You	17
After Dark	17
To Let Go or to Hold On?	18
Destiny	19
How beastly the Bourgeois is	20
Worm Either Way	22
Natural Complexion	23
The Oxford Voice	24
True Democracy	24
To be Superior	25
Swan	26
Leda	27
Give us Gods	27
Won't it be Strange?	29
Spiral Flame	30
Let the Dead bury their Dead	31
When wilt thou teach the People?	33
A Living	34
When I went to the Film	35
When I went to the Circus	35
Things Men have made	38
Things made by Iron	38
New Houses, New Clothes	38
Whatever Man makes	39
We are Transmitters	39
All that we have is Life	40
Let us be Men	40

7

	PAGE
WORK	41
WHY?	42
WHAT IS HE?	43
O! START A REVOLUTION	43
MOON MEMORY	44
THERE IS RAIN IN ME	44
DESIRE GOES DOWN INTO THE SEA	45
THE SEA, THE SEA	45
NOVEMBER BY THE SEA	46
OLD SONG	46
GOOD HUSBANDS MAKE UNHAPPY WIVES	47
FIGHT! O MY YOUNG MEN	47
IT'S EITHER YOU FIGHT OR YOU DIE	48
DON'TS	48
THE RISEN LORD	50
THE SECRET WATERS	52
BEWARE, O MY DEAR YOUNG MEN	53
OBSCENITY	55
SEX ISN'T SIN	55
THE ELEPHANT IS SLOW TO MATE	56
SEX AND TRUST	57
THE GAZELLE CALF	58
LITTLE FISH	58
THE MOSQUITO KNOWS	58
SELF-PITY	58
NEW MOON	59
SPRAY	59
SEA-WEED	59
MY ENEMY	59
TOUCH	60
NOLI ME TANGERE	60
CHASTITY	61
LET US TALK, LET US LAUGH	62
TOUCH COMES	62
LEAVE SEX ALONE	63
THE MESS OF LOVE	64
CLIMB DOWN, O LORDLY MIND	65
EGO-BOUND	67
JEALOUSY	67
FIDELITY	68

	PAGE
KNOW DEEPLY, KNOW THYSELF MORE DEEPLY	69
ALL I ASK	71
THE UNIVERSE FLOWS	71
UNDERNEATH	72
THE PRIMAL PASSIONS	73
ESCAPE	74
THE ROOT OF OUR EVIL	75
THE IGNOBLE PROCESSION	76
NO JOY IN LIFE	76
WILD THINGS IN CAPTIVITY	77
MOURNFUL YOUNG MAN	77
MONEY-MADNESS	78
KILL MONEY	79
MEN ARE NOT BAD	80
NOTTINGHAM'S NEW UNIVERSITY	80
I AM IN A NOVEL	81
NO! MR LAWRENCE!	82
RED-HERRING	82
OUR MORAL AGE	83
WHEN I READ SHAKESPEARE	84
SALT OF THE EARTH	84
FRESH WATER	85
PEACE AND WAR	85
MANY MANSIONS	85
GLORY	86
WOE	86
ATTILA	86
WHAT WOULD YOU FIGHT FOR?	87
CHOICE	87
RICHES	88
POVERTY	88
NOBLE	88
WEALTH	89
TOLERANCE	89
COMPARI	89
SICK	90
DEAD PEOPLE	90
CEREBRAL EMOTIONS	90
WELLSIAN FUTURES	91
TO WOMEN, AS FAR AS I'M CONCERNED	91

	PAGE
BLANK	91
ELDERLY DISCONTENTED WOMEN	92
OLD PEOPLE	92
THE GRUDGE OF THE OLD	93
BEAUTIFUL OLD AGE	93
COURAGE	94
DESIRE IS DEAD	95
WHEN THE RIPE FRUIT FALLS	95
ELEMENTAL	95
FIRE	96
I WISH I KNEW A WOMAN	96
TALK	97
THE EFFORT OF LOVE	97
CAN'T BE BORNE	98
MAN REACHES A POINT	98
GRASSHOPPER IS A BURDEN	98
BASTA!	98
TRAGEDY	99
AFTER ALL THE TRAGEDIES ARE OVER	99
NULLUS	100
DIES IRAE	101
DIES ILLA	102
STOP IT	102
THE DEATH OF OUR ERA	102
THE NEW WORD	104
SUN IN ME	104
BE STILL!	104
AT LAST	105
NEMESIS	106
THE OPTIMIST	106
THE THIRD THING	106
THE SANE UNIVERSE	106
FEAR OF SOCIETY IS THE ROOT OF ALL EVIL	107
GOD	107
SANE AND INSANE	107
A SANE REVOLUTION	108
ALWAYS THIS PAYING	109
POOR YOUNG THINGS	109
A PLAYED-OUT GAME	109
TRIUMPH	110

	PAGE
THE COMBATIVE SPIRIT	110
WAGES	112
YOUNG FATHERS	113
A TALE TOLD BY AN IDIOT	113
BEING ALIVE	114
SELF-PROTECTION	114
A MAN	116
LIZARD	116
RELATIVITY	116
SPACE	117
SUN-MEN	117
SUN-WOMEN	117
DEMOCRACY	118
ARISTOCRACY OF THE SUN	119
CONSCIENCE	119
THE MIDDLE CLASSES	119
IMMORALITY	120
CENSORS	120
MAN'S IMAGE	121
IMMORAL MAN	121
COWARDS	121
THINK——!	122
PEACOCK	122
PALTRY-LOOKING PEOPLE	122
TARTS	123
LATTER-DAY SINNERS	123
FATE AND THE YOUNGER GENERATION	124
AS FOR ME, I'M A PATRIOT	125
THE ROSE OF ENGLAND	125
ENGLAND IN 1929	126
LIBERTY'S OLD OLD STORY	126
NEW BROOMS	127
POLICE SPIES	127
NOW IT'S HAPPENED	127
ENERGETIC WOMEN	128
FILM PASSION	129
FEMALE COERCION	129
VOLCANIC VENUS	130
WONDERFUL SPIRITUAL WOMEN	130
POOR BIT OF A WENCH!	131

	PAGE
What ails Thee?	131
It's No Good!	132
Ships in Bottles	132
Know Thyself, and that Thou art Mortal	134
What is Man without an Income?	135
Canvassing for the Election	137
Altercation	137
Finding your Level	138
Climbing Up	140
Conundrums	142
A Rise in the World	142
Up He goes!	143
The Saddest Day	145
Prestige	146
Have done with It	148
Henriette	149
Vitality	150
Willy Wet-Leg	151
Maybe	151
Stand Up!	152
Trust	153

PANSIES

OUR DAY IS OVER

Our day is over, night comes up
shadows steal out of the earth.
Shadows, shadows
wash over our knees and splash between our thighs,
our day is done;
we wade, we wade, we stagger, darkness rushes between our
    stones,
we shall drown.

Our day is over
night comes up.

HARK IN THE DUSK!

Hark! in the dusk
voices, gurgling like water
wreathe strong weed round the knees, as the darkness
lifts us off our feet.

As the current
thrusts warm through the loins, so the little one
wildly floats, swirls,
and the flood strikes the belly, and we are gone.

ELEPHANTS IN THE CIRCUS

Elephants in the circus
have æons of weariness round their eyes.
Yet they sit up
and show vast bellies to the children.

ELEPHANTS PLODDING

Plod! Plod!
And what ages of time
the worn arches of their spines support!

ON THE DRUM

The huge old female on the drum
shuffles gingerly round
and smiles; the vastness of her elephant antiquity
is amused.

TWO PERFORMING ELEPHANTS

He stands with his forefeet on the drum
and the other, the old one, the pallid hoary female
must creep her great bulk beneath the bridge of him.

On her knees, in utmost caution
all agog, and curling up her trunk
she edges through without upsetting him.
Triumph! the ancient, pig-tailed monster!

When her trick is to climb over him
with what shadow-like slow carefulness
she skims him, sensitive
as shadows from the ages gone and perished
in touching him, and planting her round feet.

While the wispy, modern children, half-afraid
watch silent. The looming of the hoary, far-gone ages
is too much for them.

TWILIGHT

TWILIGHT
thick underdusk
and a hidden voice like water clucking
callously continuous.
While darkness submerges the stones
and splashes warm between the buttocks.

CUPS

CUPS, let them be dark
like globules of night about to go plash.
I want to drink out of dark cups that drip down on their feet.

BOWLS

TAKE away all this crystal and silver
and give me soft-skinned wood
that lives erect through long nights, physically
to put to my lips.

YOU

YOU, you don't know me.
When have your knees ever nipped me
like fire-tongs a live coal
for a minute?

AFTER DARK

CAN you, after dark, become a darkie?
Could one, at night, run up against the standing flesh of you
with a shock, as against the blackness of a negro,
and catch flesh like the night in one's arms.

TO LET GO OR TO HOLD ON——?

Shall we let go,
and allow the soul to find its level
downwards, ebbing downwards, ebbing downwards to the
    flood?
till the head floats tilted like a bottle forward tilted
on the sea, with no message in it; and the body is submerged
heavy and swaying like a whale recovering
from wounds, below the deep black wave?
like a whale recovering its velocity and strength
under the cold black wave.

Or else, or else
shall a man brace himself up
and lift his face and set his breast
and go forth to change the world?
gather his will and his energy together
and fling himself in effort after effort
upon the world, to bring a change to pass?

Tell me first, O tell me,
will the dark flood of our day's annihilation
swim deeper, deeper, till it leaves no peak emerging?
Shall we be lost, all of us
and gone like weed, like weed, like eggs of fishes,
like sperm of whales, like germs of the great dead past
into which the creative future shall blow strange, unknown
    forms?

Are we nothing, already, but the lapsing of a great dead past?
Is the best that we are but sperm, loose sperm, like the sperm
    of fishes

that drifts upon time and chaos, till some unknown future
    takes it up
and is fecund with a new Day of new creatures ? different
    from us.

Or is our shattered Argosy, our leaking ark
at this moment scraping tardy Ararat ?
Have we got to get down and clear away the debris
of a swamped civilisation, and start a new world of man
that will blossom forth the whole of human nature ?

Must we hold on, hold on
and go ahead with what is human nature
and make a new job of the human world ?

Or can we let it go ?
O, can we let it go,
and leave it to some nature that is more than human
to use the sperm of what's worth while in us
and thus eliminate us ?
is the time come for humans
now to begin to disappear,
leaving it to the vast revolutions of creative chaos
to bring forth creatures that are an improvement on humans,
as the horse was an improvement on the ichthyosaurus ?
Must we hold on ?
Or can we now let go ?

Or is it even possible we must do both ?

DESTINY

O DESTINY, destiny,
do you exist, and can a man touch your hand ?

O destiny
if I could see your hand, and it were thumbs down,
I would be willing to give way, like the pterodactyl,
and accept obliteration.
I would not even ask to leave a fossil claw extant,
nor a thumb-mark like a clue,
I would be willing to vanish completely, completely.

But if it is thumbs up, and mankind must go on being mankind,
then I am willing to fight, I will roll my sleeves up
and start in.

Only, O destiny
I wish you'd show your hand.

HOW BEASTLY THE BOURGEOIS IS——

How beastly the bourgeois is
especially the male of the species—

Presentable, eminently presentable—
shall I make you a present of him?

Isn't he handsome? isn't he healthy? Isn't he a fine specimen?
doesn't he look the fresh clean englishman, outside?
Isn't it god's own image? tramping his thirty miles a day
after partridges, or a little rubber ball?
wouldn't you like to be like that, well off, and quite the thing?

Oh, but wait!
Let him meet a new emotion, let him be faced with another man's need,

let him come home to a bit of moral difficulty, let life face
    him with a new demand on his understanding
and then watch him go soggy, like a wet meringue.
Watch him turn into a mess, either a fool or a bully.
Just watch the display of him, confronted with a new demand
    on his intelligence,
a new life-demand.

How beastly the bourgeois is
especially the male of the species—

Nicely groomed, like a mushroom
standing there so sleek and erect and eyeable—
and like a fungus, living on the remains of bygone life
sucking his life out of the dead leaves of greater life than his
    own.

And even so, he's stale, he's been there too long.
Touch him, and you'll find he's all gone inside
just like an old mushroom, all wormy inside, and hollow
under a smooth skin and an upright appearance.

Full of seething, wormy, hollow feelings
rather nasty—
How beastly the bourgeois is!

Standing in their thousands, these appearances, in damp
    England
what a pity they can't all be kicked over
like sickening toadstools, and left to melt back, swiftly
into the soil of England.

WORM EITHER WAY

If you live along with all the other people
and are just like them, and conform, and are nice
you're just a worm—

and if you live with all the other people
and you don't like them and won't be like them and won't
    conform
then you're just the worm that has turned,
in either case, a worm.

The conforming worm stays just inside the skin
respectably unseen, and cheerfully gnaws away at the heart
    of life,
making it all rotten inside.

The unconforming worm—that is, the worm that has turned—
gnaws just the same, gnawing the substance out of life,
but he insists on gnawing a little hole in the social epidermis
and poking his head out and waving himself
and saying : Look at me, I am *not* respectable,
I do all the things the bourgeois daren't do,
I booze and fornicate and use foul language and despise your
    honest man.—

But why should the worm that has turned protest so much ?
The bonnie bonnie bourgeois goes a-whoring up back streets
just the same.
The busy busy bourgeois imbibes his little share
just the same
if not more.
The pretty pretty bourgeois pinks his language just as pink

if not pinker,
and in private boasts his exploits even louder, if you ask me,
than the other.
While as to honesty, Oh look where the money lies!

So I can't see where the worm that has turned puts anything
    over
the worm that is too cunning to turn.
On the contrary, he merely gives himself away.
The turned worm shouts: I bravely booze!
the other says: Have one with me!
The turned worm boasts: I copulate!
the unturned says: You look it.
You're a d—— b—— b—— p—— bb——, says the worm
    that's turned.
Quite! says the other. Cuckoo!

NATURAL COMPLEXION

BUT you see, said the handsome young man with the chamois
    gloves
to the woman rather older than himself,
if you don't use rouge and a lip-stick, in Paris
they'll take you for a woman of the people.

So spoke the british gentleman
pulling on his chamois gloves
and using his most melodious would-be-oxford voice.

And the woman said: Dear me!
how rough that would be on you, darling!
Only, if you insist on pulling on those chamois gloves
I swear I'll pull off my knickers, right in the Rue de la Paix.

THE OXFORD VOICE

When you hear it languishing
and hooing and cooing and sidling through the front teeth,
   the oxford voice
    or worse still
   the would-be oxford voice
you don't even laugh any more, you can't.

For every blooming bird is an oxford cuckoo nowadays,
you can't sit on a bus nor in the tube
but it breathes gently and languishingly in the back of your
 neck.

And oh, so seductively superior, so seductively
   self-effacingly
   deprecatingly
   superior.—
We wouldn't insist on it for a moment
   but we are
    we are
   you admit we are
    superior.——

TRUE DEMOCRACY

I wish I was a gentleman
as full of wet as a watering-can
to whizz in the eye of a police-man—

But my dear fellow, my dear fellow
can it be that you still don't know
that every man, whether high or low
is a gentleman if he thinks himself so?—

He is an' all, you bet 'e is!
I bet I am.—You can 'old yer phiz
abaht it.—Yes, I'm a gent, an' Liz
'ere, she's a lidy, aren't yer, old quizz?—

Of course I'm a lidy, what d'yer think?
You mind who yer sayin' isn't lidies!
All the hinglish is gentlemen an' lidies,
like the King an' Queen, though they're up just a wink.—

—Of course you are, but let me say
I'm American, from New Orleans,
and in my country, just over the way,
we are *all* kings and queens!—

TO BE SUPERIOR

How nice it is to be superior!
Because really, it's no use pretending, one *is* superior, isn't one?
I mean people like you and me.—

Quite! I quite agree.
The trouble is, everybody thinks they're just as superior
as we are; just as superior.—

That's what's so boring! people are so boring.
But they can't really think it, do you think?
At the bottom, they must *know* we are really superior
don't you think?
don't you think, *really*, they *know* we're their superiors?—

I couldn't say.
I've never got to the bottom of superiority.
I should like to.

SWAN

FAR-OFF
at the core of space
at the quick
of time
beats
and goes still
the great swan upon the waters of all endings
the swan within vast chaos, within the electron.

For us
no longer he swims calmly
nor clacks across the forces furrowing a great gay trail
of happy energy,
nor is he nesting passive upon the atoms,
nor flying north desolative icewards
to the sleep of ice,
nor feeding in the marshes,
nor honking horn-like into the twilight.—

But he stoops, now
in the dark
upon us;
he is treading our women
and we men are put out
as the vast white bird
furrows our featherless women
with unknown shocks
and stamps his black marsh-feet on their white and marshy flesh

LEDA

COME not with kisses
not with caresses
of hands and lips and murmurings;
come with a hiss of wings
and sea-touch tip of a beak
and treading of wet, webbed, wave-working feet
into the marsh-soft belly.

GIVE US GODS

GIVE us gods, Oh give them us!
Give us gods.
We are so tired of men
and motor-power.—

But not god grey-bearded and dictatorial,
nor yet that pale young man afraid of fatherhood
shelving substance on to the woman, Madonna mia! shabby
    virgin!
nor gusty Jove, with his eye on immortal tarts,
nor even the musical, suave young fellow
wooing boys and beauty.

Give us gods
give us something else—

Beyond the great bull that bellowed through space, and got
    his throat cut.
Beyond even that eagle, that phœnix, hanging over the gold
    egg of all things,
further still, before the curled horns of the ram stepped forth

or the stout swart beetle rolled the globe of dung in which man
    should hatch,
or even the sly gold serpent fatherly lifted his head off the
    earth to think—

Give us gods before these—
Thou shalt have other gods before these.

Where the waters end in marshes
swims the wild swan
sweeps the high goose above the mists
honking in the gloom the honk of procreation from such
    throats.

Mists
where the electron behaves and misbehaves as it will,
where the forces tie themselves up into knots of atoms
and come untied;
mists
of mistiness complicated into knots and clots that barge about
and bump on one another and explode into more mist, or don't,
mist of energy most scientific—
But give us gods!

Look then
where the father of all things swims in a mist of atoms
electrons and energies, quantums and relativities
mists, wreathing mists,
like a wild swan, or a goose, whose honk goes through my
    bladder.

And in the dark unscientific I feel the drum-winds of his wings
and the drip of his cold, webbed feet, mud-black

brush over my face as he goes
to seek the women in the dark, our women, our weird women
    whom he treads
with dreams and thrusts that make them cry in their sleep.

Gods, do you ask for gods?
Where there is woman there is swan.

Do you think, scientific man, you'll be father of your own
    babies?
Don't imagine it.
There'll be babies born that are cygnets, O my soul!
young wild swans!
And babies of women will come out young wild geese, O my
    heart!
the geese that saved Rome, and will lose London.

WON'T IT BE STRANGE——?

WON'T it be strange, when the nurse brings the new-born infant
to the proud father, and shows its little, webbed greenish feet
made to smite the waters behind it?
or the round, wild vivid eye of a wild-goose staring
out of fathomless skies and seas?
or when it utters that undaunted little bird-cry
of one who will settle on ice-bergs, and honk across the Nile?—

And when the father says: This is none of mine!
Woman, where got you this little beast?—
will there be a whistle of wings in the air, and an icy draught?
will the singing of swans, high up, high up, invisible
break the drums of his ears
and leave him forever listening for the answer?

SPIRAL FLAME

THERE have been so many gods
that now there are none.
When the One God made a monopoly of it
he wore us out, so now we are godless and unbelieving.

Yet, O my young men, there is a vivifier.
There is that which makes us eager.
While we are eager, we think nothing of it.
Sum ergo non cogito.
But when our eagerness leaves us, we are godless and full of
    thought.

We have worn out the gods, and they us.
That pale one, filled with renunciation and pain and white love
has worn us weary of renunciation and love and even pain.
That strong one, ruling the universe with a rod of iron
has sickened us thoroughly with rods of iron and rulers and
    strong men.
The All-wise has tired us of wisdom.
The weeping mother of god, inconsolable over her son
makes us prefer to be womanless, rather than be wept over.
And that poor late makeshift, Aphrodite emerging in a bathing-
    suit from our modern sea-side foam
has successfully killed all desire in us whatsoever.

Yet, O my young men, there is a vivifier.
There is a swan-like flame that curls round the centre of space
and flutters at the core of the atom,
there is a spiral flame-tip that can lick our little atoms into
        fusion

so we roar up like bonfires of vitality
and fuse in a broad hard flame of many men in a oneness.

O pillars of flame by night, O my young men
spinning and dancing like flamey fire-spouts in the dark ahead
    of the multitude!
O ruddy god in our veins, O fiery god in our genitals!
O rippling hard fire of courage, O fusing of hot trust
when the fire reaches us, O my young men!

And the same flame that fills us with life, it will dance and
    burn the house down,
all the fittings and elaborate furnishings
and all the people that go with the fittings and the furnishings,
the upholstered dead that sit in deep arm-chairs.

LET THE DEAD BURY THEIR DEAD——

Let the dead go bury their dead
don't help them.
Let the dead look after the dead
leave them to one another,
don't serve them.

The dead in their nasty dead hands
have heaps of money,
don't take it.

The dead in their seething minds
have phosphorescent teeming white words
of putrescent wisdom and sapience that subtly stinks;
don't ever believe them.

The dead are in myriads, they seem mighty.
They make trains chuff, motor-cars titter, ships lurch,
mills grind on and on,
and keep you in millions at the mills, sightless pale slaves,
pretending these are the mills of God.

It is the great lie of the dead.
The mills of industry are not the mills of God.
And the mills of God grind otherwise, with the winds of life
    for the mill-stones.
Trust the mills of God, though they grind exceeding small.
But as for the mills of men
don't be harnessed to them.

The dead give ships and engines, cinema, radio and gramo-
    phone,
they send aeroplanes across the sky,
and they say: Now, behold, you are living the great life!
While you listen in, while you watch the film, while you drive
    the car,
while you read about the air-ship crossing the wild Atlantic
behold, you are living the great life, the stupendous life!—

As you know, it is a complete lie.
You are all going dead and corpse-pale
listening in to the lie.
Spit it out.

O cease to listen to the living dead.
They are only greedy for your life!
O cease to labour for the gold-toothed dead,

they are so greedy, yet so helpless if not worked for.
Don't ever be kind to the smiling, tooth-mouthed dead
don't ever be kind to the dead
it is pandering to corpses,
the repulsive, living fat dead.

Bury a man gently if he has lain down and died.
But with the walking and talking and conventionally persuasive dead
with bank accounts and insurance policies
don't sympathise, or you taint the unborn babes.

WHEN WILT THOU TEACH THE PEOPLE——?

WHEN wilt thou teach the people,
God of justice, to save themselves—?
They have been saved so often
and sold.

O God of justice, send no more saviours
of the people!

When a saviour has saved a people
they find he has sold them to his father.
They say: We are saved, but we are starving.
He says: The sooner will you eat imaginary cake in the mansions of my father.
They say: Can't we have a loaf of common bread?
He says: No, you must go to heaven, and eat the most marvellous cake.—

Or Napoleon says: Since I have saved you from the ci-devants,
you are my property, be prepared to die for me, and to work
    for me.—

Or later republicans say: You are saved,
therefore you are our savings, our capital
with which we shall do big business.—

Or Lenin says: You are saved, but you are saved wholesale.
You are no longer men, that is bourgeois;
you are items in the soviet state,
and each item will get its ration,
but it is the soviet state alone which counts
the items are of small importance,
the state having saved them all.—

And so it goes on, with the saving of the people.
God of justice, when wilt thou teach them to save themselves?

A LIVING

A MAN should never earn his living,
if he earns his life he'll be lovely.

A bird
picks up its seeds or little snails
between heedless earth and heaven
in heedlessness.

But, the plucky little sport, it gives to life
song, and chirruping, gay feathers, fluff-shadowed warmth
and all the unspeakable charm of birds hopping and fluttering
    and being birds.
—And we, we get it all from them for nothing.

WHEN I WENT TO THE FILM——

When I went to the film, and saw all the black-and-white
　　feelings that nobody felt,
and heard the audience sighing and sobbing with all the
　　emotions they none of them felt,
and saw them cuddling with rising passions they none of them
　　for a moment felt,
and caught them moaning from close-up kisses, black-and-
　　white kisses that could not be felt,
it was like being in heaven, which I am sure has a white
　　atmosphere
upon which shadows of people, pure personalities
are cast in black and white, and move
in flat ecstasy, supremely unfelt,
and heavenly.

WHEN I WENT TO THE CIRCUS——

When I went to the circus that had pitched on the waste lot
it was full of uneasy people
frightened of the bare earth and the temporary canvas
and the smell of horses and other beasts
instead of merely the smell of man.

Monkeys rode rather grey and wizened
on curly plump piebald ponies
and the children uttered a little cry—
and dogs jumped through hoops and turned somersaults
and then the geese scuttled in in a little flock
and round the ring they went to the sound of the whip
then doubled, and back, with a funny up-flutter of wings—
and the children suddenly shouted out.

Then came the hush again, like a hush of fear.

The tight-rope lady, pink and blonde and nude-looking, with
    a few gold spangles
footed cautiously out on the rope, turned prettily, spun round
bowed, and lifted her foot in her hand, smiled, swung her
    parasol
to another balance, tripped round, poised, and slowly sank
her handsome thighs down, down, till she slept her splendid
    body on the rope.
When she rose, tilting her parasol, and smiled at the cautious
    people
they cheered, but nervously.

The trapeze man, slim and beautiful and like a fish in the air
swung great curves through the upper space, and came down
    like a star
—And the people applauded, with hollow, frightened applause.

The elephants, huge and grey, loomed their curved bulk
    through the dusk
and sat up, taking strange postures, showing the pink soles of
    their feet
and curling their precious live trunks like ammonites
and moving always with soft slow precision
as when a great ship moves to anchor.
The people watched and wondered, and seemed to resent the
    mystery that lies in beasts.

Horse, gay horses, swirling round and plaiting
in a long line, their heads laid over each other's necks;

they were happy, they enjoyed it;
all the creatures seemed to enjoy the game
in the circus, with their circus people.

But the audience, compelled to wonder
compelled to admire the bright rhythms of moving bodies
compelled to see the delicate skill of flickering human bodies
flesh flamey and a little heroic, even in a tumbling clown,
they were not really happy.
There was no gushing response, as there is at the film.

When modern people see the carnal body dauntless and flickering gay
playing among the elements neatly, beyond competition
and displaying no personality,
modern people are depressed.

Modern people feel themselves at a disadvantage.
They know they have no bodies that could play among the elements.
They have only their personalities, that are best seen flat, on the film,
flat personalities in two dimensions, imponderable and touchless.

And they grudge the circus people the swooping gay weight of limbs
that flower in mere movement,
and they grudge them the immediate, physical understanding they have with their circus beasts,
and they grudge them their circus-life altogether.

Yet the strange, almost frightened shout of delight that comes
    now and then from the children
shows that the children vaguely know how cheated they are
    of their birthright
in the bright wild circus flesh.

THINGS MEN HAVE MADE——

Things men have made with wakened hands, and put soft
    life into
are awake through years with transferred touch, and go on
    glowing
for long years.
And for this reason, some old things are lovely
warm still with the life of forgotten men who made them.

THINGS MADE BY IRON——

Things made by iron and handled by steel
are born dead, they are shrouds, they soak life out of us.
Till after a long time, when they are old and have steeped in
    our life
they begin to be soothed and soothing: then we throw them
    away.

NEW HOUSES, NEW CLOTHES——

New houses, new furniture, new streets, new clothes, new
    sheets
everything new and machine-made sucks life out of us
and makes us cold, makes us lifeless
the more we have.

WHATEVER MAN MAKES——

WHATEVER man makes and makes it live
lives because of the life put into it.
A yard of India muslin is alive with Hindu life.
And a Navajo woman, weaving her rug in the pattern of her
    dream
must run the pattern out in a little break at the end
so that her soul can come out, back to her.

But in the odd pattern, like snake-marks on the sand
it leaves its trail.

WE ARE TRANSMITTERS——

As we live, we are transmitters of life.
And when we fail to transmit life, life fails to flow through us.

That is part of the mystery of sex, it is a flow onwards.
Sexless people transmit nothing.

And if, as we work, we can transmit life into our work,
life, still more life, rushes into us to compensate, to be ready
and we ripple with life through the days.

Even if it is a woman making an apple dumpling, or a man a
    stool,
if life goes into the pudding, good is the pudding
good is the stool,
content is the woman, with fresh life rippling in to her,
content is the man.

Give, and it shall be given unto you
is still the truth about life.
But giving life is not so easy.
It doesn't mean handing it out to some mean fool, or letting the living dead eat you up.
It means kindling the life-quality where it was not,
even if it's only in the whiteness of a washed pocket-handkerchief.

ALL THAT WE HAVE IS LIFE——

ALL that we have, while we live, is life;
and if you don't live during your life, you are a piece of dung.

And work is life, and life is lived in work
unless you're a wage-slave.
While a wage-slave works, he leaves life aside
and stands there a piece of dung.

Men should refuse to be lifelessly at work.
Men should refuse to be heaps of wage-earning dung.
Men should refuse to work at all, as wage-slaves.
Men should demand to work for themselves, of themselves,
    and put their life in it.
For if a man has no life in his work, he is mostly a heap of dung.

LET US BE MEN——

FOR God's sake, let us be men
not monkeys minding machines
or sitting with our tails curled
while the machine amuses us, the radio or film or gramophone.

Monkeys with a bland grin on our faces.—

WORK

THERE is no point in work
unless it absorbs you
like an absorbing game.

If it doesn't absorb you
if it's never any fun,
don't do it.

When a man goes out into his work
he is alive like a tree in spring,
he is living, not merely working.

When the Hindus weave thin wool into long, long lengths of stuff
with their thin dark hands and their wide dark eyes and their still souls absorbed
they are like slender trees putting forth leaves, a long white web of living leaf,
the tissue they weave,
and they clothe themselves in white as a tree clothes itself
in its own foliage.

As with cloth, so with houses, ships, shoes, wagons or cups or loaves
men might put them forth as a snail its shell, as a bird that leans
its breast against its nest, to make it round,
as the turnip models his round root, as the bush makes flowers and gooseberries,
putting them forth, not manufacturing them,
and cities might be as once they were, bowers grown out from the busy bodies of people.

And so it will be again, men will smash the machines.

At last, for the sake of clothing himself in his own leaf-like cloth
tissued from his life,
and dwelling in his own bowery house, like a beaver's nibbled mansion
and drinking from cups that came off his fingers like flowers off their five-fold stem,
he will cancel the machines we have got.

WHY——?

WHY have money?
why have a financial system to strangle us all in its octopus arms?
why have industry?
why have the industrial system?
why have machines, that we only have to serve?
why have a soviet, that only wants to screw us all in as parts of the machine?
why have working classes at all, as if men were only embodied jobs?
why not have men as men, and the work as merely part of the game of life?

True, we've got all these things
industrial and financial systems, machines and soviets, working classes.
But why go on having them, if they belittle us?
Why should we be belittled any longer?

WHAT IS HE?

WHAT is he?
—A man, of course.
Yes, but what does he do?
—He lives and is a man.
Oh quite! But he must work. He must have a job of some
    sort.
—Why?
Because obviously he's not one of the leisured classes.
—I don't know. He has lots of leisure. And he makes quite
    beautiful chairs.—
There you are then! He's a cabinet maker.
—No no!
Anyhow a carpenter and joiner.
—Not at all.
But you said so.
—What did I say?
That he made chairs, and was a joiner and carpenter.
—I said he made chairs, but I did not say he was a carpenter.
All right then, he's just an amateur.
—Perhaps! Would you say a thrush was a professional
    flautist, or just an amateur?—
I'd say it was just a bird.
—And I say he is just a man.
All right! You always did quibble.

O! START A REVOLUTION——

O! START a revolution, somebody!
not to get the money
but to lose it all for ever.

O! start a revolution, somebody!
not to install the working classes
but to abolish the working classes for ever
and have a world of men.

MOON MEMORY

When the moon falls on a man's blood
white and slippery, as on the black water in a port
shaking asunder, and flicking at his ribs—

then the noisy, dirty day-world
exists no more, nor ever truly existed;
but instead
this wet white gleam
twitches, and ebbs hitting, washing inwardly, silverily against
    his ribs
on his soul that is dark ocean within him.

And under the flicking of the white whip-lash of the moon
sea-beasts immersed lean sideways and flash bright
in pure brilliance of anger, sea-immersed anger
at the trashy, motor-driven transit of dirty day
that has left scum on the sea, even in the night.

THERE IS RAIN IN ME——

There is rain in me
running down, running down, trickling
away from memory.

There is ocean in me
swaying, swaying, O so deep
so fathomlessly black

and spurting suddenly up, snow-white, like snow-leopards
    rearing
high and clawing with rage at the cliffs of the soul
then disappearing back with a hiss
of eternal salt rage; angry is old ocean within a man.

DESIRE GOES DOWN INTO THE SEA——

I HAVE no desire any more
towards woman or man, bird, beast or creature or thing.

All day long I feel the tide rocking, rocking
though it strikes no shore
in me.

Only mid-ocean.—

THE SEA, THE SEA——

THE sea dissolves so much
and the moon makes away with so much more than we know—

Once the moon comes down
and the sea gets hold of us
cities dissolve like rock-salt
and the sugar melts out of life
iron washes away like an old blood-stain
gold goes out into a green shadow
money makes even no sediment
and only the heart
glitters in salty triumph
over all it has known, that has gone now into salty nothingness.

45

NOVEMBER BY THE SEA——

Now in November nearer comes the sun
down the abandoned heaven.

As the dark closes round him, he draws nearer
as if for our company.

At the base of the lower brain
the sun in me declines to his winter solstice
and darts a few gold rays
back to the old year's sun across the sea.

A few gold rays thickening down to red
as the sun of my soul is setting
setting fierce and undaunted, wintry
but setting, setting behind the sounding sea between my ribs

The wide sea wins, and the dark
winter, and the great day-sun, and the sun in my soul
sinks, sinks to setting and the winter solstice
downward, they race in decline
my sun, and the great gold sun.

OLD SONG

The day is ending, the night descending,
the heart is frozen, the spirit dead;
but the moon is wending her way, attending
to other things that are left unsaid.

GOOD HUSBANDS MAKE UNHAPPY WIVES

Good husbands make unhappy wives
so do bad husbands, just as often;
but the unhappiness of a wife with a good husband
is much more devastating
than the unhappiness of a wife with a bad husband.

FIGHT! O MY YOUNG MEN——

Fight! don't you feel you're fading
into slow death?
Fight then, poor duffers degrading
your very breath.

Open your half-dead eyes
you half-alive young,
look round and realise
the muck from which you've sprung.

The money-muck, you simple flowers
of your forefathers' muck-heap;
and the money-muck-worms, the extant powers
that have got you in keep.

Old money-worms, young money-worms
money-worm professors
spinning a glamour round money, and clergymen
lifting a bank-book to bless us!

In the odour of lucrative sanctity
stand they—and god, how they stink!
Rise then, my young men, rise at them!
Or if you can't rise, just think—

Think of the world that you're stifling in,
think what a world it might be!
Think of the rubbish you're trifling in
with enfeebled vitality!

And then, if you amount to a hill o' beans
start in and bust it all;
money, hypocrisy, greed, machines
that have ground you so small.

IT'S EITHER YOU FIGHT OR YOU DIE——

It's either you fight or you die,
young gents, you've got no option.
No good asking the reason why
it's either you fight or you die,
die, die, lily-liveredly die
or fight and make the splinters fly
bust up the holy apple-pie
you've got no option.

Don't say you can't, start in and try:
give great hypocrisy the lie
and tackle the blowsy big blow-fly
of money; do it or die!
You've got no option.

DON'TS

Fight your little fight, my boy,
fight and be a man.
Don't be a good little, good little boy
being as good as you can

and agreeing with all the mealy-mouthed, mealy-mouthed
truths that the sly trot out
to protect themselves and their greedy-mouthed, greedy
    mouthed
cowardice, every old lout.

Don't live up to the dear little girl who costs
you your manhood, and makes you pay.
Nor the dear old mater who so proudly boasts
that you'll make your way.

Don't earn golden opinions, opinions golden,
or at least worth Treasury notes,
from all sorts of men; don't be beholden
to the herd inside the pen.

Don't long to have dear little, dear little boys
whom you'll have to educate
to earn their living; nor yet girls, sweet joys
who will find it so hard to mate.

Nor a dear little home, with its cost, its cost
that you have to pay,
earning your living while your life is lost
and dull death comes in a day.

Don't be sucked in by the su-superior,
don't swallow the culture bait,
don't drink, don't drink and get beerier and beerier,
do learn to discriminate.

Do hold yourself together, and fight
with a hit-hit here and a hit-hit there,
and a comfortable feeling at night
that you've let in a little air.

A little fresh air in the money sty,
knocked a little hole in the holy prison,
done your own little bit, made your own little try
that the risen Christ should *be* risen.

THE RISEN LORD

THE risen lord, the risen lord
has risen in the flesh,
and treads the earth to feel the soil
though his feet are still nesh.

The risen lord, the risen lord
has opened his eyes afresh,
and sees strange looks on the faces of men
all held in leash.

And he says: I never have seen them before,
these people of flesh;
these are no spirits caught and sore
in the physical mesh.

They are substance itself, that flows in thick
flame of flesh forever travelling
like the flame of a candle, slow and quick
fluttering and softly unravelling.

It moves, it ripples, and all the time
it changes, and with it change
moods, thoughts, desires, and deeds that chime
with the rippling fleshly change.

I never saw them, how they must soften
themselves with oil, and lard
their guts with a certain fat, and often
laugh, and laugh hard.

If they didn't, if they did not soften
themselves with oil, and lard
their guts with a certain fat, and often
laugh, and laugh hard

they would not be men, and they must be men;
they *are* their own flesh.—I lay
in the tomb and was not; I have risen again
to look the other way.

Lo! I am flesh, and the blood that races
is me in the narrows of my wrists.
Lo, I see fear in the twisted faces
of men, they clench fear in their fists!

Lo! on the other side the grave
I have conquered the fear of death,
but the fear of life is still here; I am brave
yet I fear my own breath.

Now I must conquer the fear of life,
the knock of the blood in my wrists,
the breath that rushes through my nose, the strife
of desires in the loins' dark twists.

What do you want, wild loins ? and what
do you want, warm heart ? and what
wide eyes and wondering spirit ?—not
death, no not death for your lot !

They ask, and they must be answered ; they
are, and they shall be, to the end.
Lo ! there is woman, and her way is a strange way
I must follow also her trend.

I died, and death is neuter ; it speaks not, it gives
no answer ; man rises again
with mouth and loins and needs, he lives
again man among men.

So it is, so it will be, for ever and ever.
And still the great needs of men
will clamour forth from the flesh, and never
can denial deny them again.

THE SECRET WATERS

What was lost is found
what was wounded is sound,
the key of life on the bodies of men
unlocks the fountains of peace again.

The fountains of peace, the fountains of peace
well softly up for a new increase,
but they bubble under the heavy wall
of this house of life that encloses us all.

They bubble under the heavy wall
that was once a house, and is now a prison,
and never a one among us all
knows that the waters have risen.

None of us knows, O none of us knows
the welling of peace when it rises and flows
in secret under the sickening wall
of the prison house that encloses us all.

And we shall not know, we shall not know
till the secret waters overflow
and loosen the brick and the hard cement
of the walls within which our lives are spent.

Till the walls begin to loosen and crack,
to gape, and our house is going to wrack
and ruin above us, and the crash of release
is death to us all, in the marshes of peace.

BEWARE, O MY DEAR YOUNG MEN—

BEWARE, O my dear young men, of going rotten.
    It's so easy to follow suit;
people in their thirties, and the older ones, have gotten
    bad inside, like fruit
that nobody eats and nobody wants, so it rots, but is not
    forgotten.

Rotten inside, they are, and seething
    with small obscenities;
and they whisper it out, and they titter it out, breathing
    among soft amenities,
a vapour of rottenness out of their mouths, like sewer-stench
    wreathing.

And it's funny, my dear young men, that you in your twenties
    should love the sewer scent
of obscenity, and lift your noses where the vent is
    and run towards it, bent
on smelling it all, before your bit of vitality spent is.

For obscenity, after all, my dear young men
    is only mental dirt,
the dirty mind like a urinal again
    or a dung squirt;
and I thought you wanted life and experience, dear young
    men!

All this obscenity is just mental, mental, mental,
    it's the village-idiot mind
playing with muck; and I thought you young gents experi-
    mental
    were out to find
new life for yourselves and your women, complemental.

But if obscene village idiots you want to be, then be it.
    But don't imagine you'll get
satisfactory experience from it; can't you see it?
    the idiot with his chin all wet
goggling obscenities! If that's you and your fate, why then,
    dree it.

OBSCENITY

THE body of itself is clean, but the caged mind
is a sewer inside, it pollutes, O it pollutes
the guts and the stones and the womb, rots them down, leaves
    a rind
of maquillage and pose and malice to shame the brutes.

SEX ISN'T SIN——

SEX isn't sin, ah no! sex isn't sin,
nor is it dirty, not until the dirty mind pokes in.

We shall do as we like, sin is obsolete, the young assert.
Sin is obsolete, sin is obsolete, but not so dirt.

And sex, alas, gets dirtier and dirtier, worked from the mind.
Sex gets dirtier and dirtier, the more it is fooled with, we find.

And dirt, if it isn't sin, is worse, especially dirt inside.
If you're dirty inside you go rotten, and once rotten, woe
    betide!

Sex isn't sin, but dirty sex is worse, so there you are!
Why don't you know what's what, young people? Seems to
    me you're far

duller than your grandmothers. But leave that aside.
Let's be honest at last about sex, or show at least that we've
    tried.

Sex isn't sin, it's a delicate flow between women and men,
and the sin is to damage the flow, force it or dirty it or suppress
    it again.

Sex isn't something you've got to play with; sex is *you*.
It's the flow of your life, it's your moving self, and you are due
to be true to the nature of it, its reserve, its sensitive pride
that it always has to begin with, and by which you ought to
    abide.

Know yourself, O know yourself, that you are mortal; and
    know
the sensitive delicacy of your sex, in its ebbing to and fro,
and the mortal reserve of your sex, as it stays in your depths
    below.

And don't, with the nasty, prying mind, drag it out from its
    deeps
and finger it and force it, and shatter the rhythm it keeps
when it's left alone, as it stirs and rouses and sleeps.

O know yourself, O know your sex! You must know, there
    is no escape.
You must know sex in order to save it, your deepest self,
    from the rape
of the itching mind and the mental self, with its pruriency
    always agape.

THE ELEPHANT IS SLOW TO MATE——

The elephant, the huge old beast,
    is slow to mate;
he finds a female, they show no haste
    they wait

for the sympathy in their vast shy hearts
    slowly, slowly to rouse
as they loiter along the river-beds
    and drink and browse

and dash in panic through the brake
    of forest with the herd,
and sleep in massive silence, and wake
    together, without a word.

So slowly the great hot elephant hearts
    grow full of desire,
and the great beasts mate in secret at last,
    hiding their fire.

Oldest they are and the wisest of beasts
    so they know at last
how to wait for the loneliest of feasts
    for the full repast.

They do not snatch, they do not tear;
    their massive blood
moves as the moon-tides, near, more near,
    till they touch in flood.

SEX AND TRUST

If you want to have sex, you've got to trust
at the core of your heart, the other creature
The other creature, the other creature
not merely the personal upstart;

but the creature there, that has come to meet you
trust it you must, you must
or the experience amounts to nothing,
mere evacuation-lust.

THE GAZELLE CALF

THE gazelle calf, O my children,
goes behind its mother across the desert,
goes behind its mother on blithe bare foot
requiring no shoes, O my children!

LITTLE FISH

THE tiny fish enjoy themselves
in the sea.
Quick little splinters of life,
their little lives are fun to them
in the sea.

THE MOSQUITO KNOWS——

THE mosquito knows full well, small as he is
he's a beast of prey.
But after all
he only takes his bellyful,
he doesn't put my blood in the bank.

SELF-PITY

I NEVER saw a wild thing
sorry for itself.
A small bird will drop frozen dead from a bough
without ever having felt sorry for itself.

NEW MOON

The new moon, of no importance
lingers behind as the yellow sun glares and is gone beyond the
    sea's edge;
earth smokes blue;
the new moon, in cool height above the blushes,
brings a fresh fragrance of heaven to our senses.

SPRAY

It is a wonder foam is so beautiful.
A wave bursts in anger on a rock, broken up
in wild white sibilant spray
and falls back, drawing in its breath with rage,
with frustration how beautiful!

SEA-WEED

Sea-weed sways and sways and swirls
as if swaying were its form of stillness;
and if it flushes against fierce rock
it slips over it as shadows do, without hurting itself.

MY ENEMY

If it is a question of him or me
then down with him!

If he is not with me but against me,
if his presence and his breath are poison to me,
then, if he comes near me
down with him.

Down with him
to the pit of annihilation.

But if he stays far from me, and does not touch me,
he is no longer my concern, he ceases to be
my enemy.

TOUCH

SINCE we have become so cerebral
we can't bear to touch or be touched.

Since we are so cerebral
we are humanly out of touch.

And so we must remain.
For if, cerebrally, we force ourselves into touch, into contact
physical and fleshly,
we violate ourselves,
we become vicious.

NOLI ME TANGERE——

NOLI me tangere, touch me not!
O you creatures of mind, don't touch me!
O you with mental fingers, O never put your hand on me!
O you with mental bodies, stay a little distance from me!

And let us, if you will, talk and mingle
in mental contact, gay and sad.
But only that.
O don't confuse
the body into it, let us stay apart.

Great is my need to be chaste
and apart, in this cerebral age.
Great is my need to be untouched,
untouched.
Noli me tangere!

CHASTITY

CHASTITY, beloved chastity,
O beloved chastity,
how infinitely dear to me
chastity, beloved chastity!

That my body need not be
fingered by the mind,
or prostituted by the dree
contact of cerebral flesh—

O leave me clean from mental fingering
from the cold copulation of the will,
from all the white, self-conscious lechery
the modern mind calls love!

From all the mental poetry
of deliberate love-making,
from all the false felicity
of deliberately taking

the body of another unto mine,
O God deliver me!
leave me alone, let me be!

Chastity, dearer far to me
than any contact that can be
in this mind-mischievous age!

LET US TALK, LET US LAUGH

Let us talk, let us laugh, let us tell
all kinds of things to one another;
men and women, let us be
gay and amusing together, and free
from airs and from false modesty.

But at the same time, don't let's think
that this quite real intimacy
of talk and thought and me-and-thee
means anything further and physical.

Nay, on the very contrary,
all this talking intimacy
is only real and right if we
keep ourselves separate physically
and quite apart.

To proceed from mental intimacy
to physical is just messy,
and really, a nasty violation,
and the ruin of any decent relation
between us.—

TOUCH COMES——

Touch comes when the white mind sleeps
and only then.

Touch comes slowly, if ever; it seeps
slowly up in the blood of men
and women.

Soft slow sympathy
of the blood in me, of the blood in thee
rises and flushes insidiously
over the conscious personality
of each of us, and covers us
with a soft one warmth, and a generous
kindled togetherness, so we go
into each other as tides flow
under a moon they do now know.

Personalities exist apart;
and personal intimacy has no heart.
Touch is of the blood
uncontaminated, the unmental flood.

When again in us
the soft blood softly flows together
towards touch, then this delirious
day of the mental welter and blether
will be passing away, we shall cease to fuss.

LEAVE SEX ALONE——

LEAVE sex alone, leave sex alone, let it die right away,
let it die right away, till it rises of itself again.

Meanwhile, if we must, let us think about it, and talk about it
straight, to the very end,
since the need is on us.

But while we think of it, and talk of it
let us leave it alone, physically, keep apart.
For while we have sex in the mind, we truly have none in the
    body.

Sex is a state of grace
and you'll have to wait.
You'll even have to repent.
And in some strange and silent way
you'll have to pray to the far-off gods
to grant it you.

At present, sex is the mind's preoccupation,
and in the body we can only mentally fornicate.
To-day, we've got no sex.
We have only cerebral excitations.

The mind will have to glut itself,
and the ego will have to burst like the swollen frog,
and then perhaps we shall know true sex, in ourselves.

THE MESS OF LOVE

WE'VE made a great mess of love
since we made an ideal of it.

The moment I swear to love a woman, a certain woman, all
    my life
that moment I begin to hate her.

The moment I even say to a woman: I love you!—
my love dies down considerably.

The moment love is an understood thing between us, we are sure of it,
it's a cold egg, it isn't love any more.

Love is like a flower, it must flower and fade;
if it doesn't fade, it is not a flower,
it's either an artificial rag blossom, or an immortelle, for the cemetery.

The moment the mind interferes with love, or the will fixes on it,
or the personality assumes it as an attribute, or the ego takes possession of it,
it is not love any more, it's just a mess.
And we've made a great mess of love, mind-perverted, will-perverted, ego-perverted love.

CLIMB DOWN, O LORDLY MIND——

CLIMB down, O lordly mind!
O eagle of the mind, alas, you are more like a buzzard.

Come down now, from your pre-eminence, O mind, O lofty spirit!
Your hour has struck
your unique day is over.
Absolutism is finished, in the human consciousness too.

A man is many things, he is not only a mind.
But in his consciousness, he is two-fold at least:
he is cerebral, intellectual, mental, spiritual,
but also he is instinctive, intuitive, and in touch.

The mind, that needs to know all things
must needs at last come to know its own limits,
even its own nullity, beyond a certain point.

Know thyself, and that thou art mortal,
and therefore, that thou art forever unknowable;
the mind can never reach thee.

Thou art like the moon,
and the white mind shines on one side of thee
but the other side is dark forever,
and the dark moon draws the tides also.

Thou art like the day
but thou art also like the night,
and thy darkness is forever invisible,
for the strongest light throws also the darkest shadow

The blood knows in darkness, and forever dark,
in touch, by intuition, instinctively.
The blood also knows religiously,
and of this, the mind is incapable.
The mind is non-religious.

To my dark heart, gods *are*.
In my dark heart, love is and is not.
But to my white mind
gods and love alike are but an idea,
a kind of fiction.

Man is an alternating consciousness.
Man is an alternating consciousness.

Only that exists which exists in my own consciousness.
Cogito, ergo sum.
Only that exists which exists dynamically and unmentalised
    in my blood.
Non cogito, ergo sum.
I am, I do not think I am.

EGO-BOUND

As a plant becomes pot-bound
man becomes ego-bound
enclosed in his own limited mental consciousness.

Then he can't feel any more
or love, or rejoice or even grieve any more,
he is ego-bound,
pot-bound
in the pot of his own conceit,
and he can only slowly die.

Unless he is a sturdy plant.
Then he can burst the pot,
shell off his ego
and get his roots in earth again,
raw earth.

JEALOUSY

THE jealousy of an ego-bound woman
is hideous and fearful,
it is so much stronger than her love could ever be.

The jealousy of an ego-bound woman
is a fearful thing to behold.
The ego revealed in all its monstrous inhumanity

FIDELITY

FIDELITY and love are two different things, like a flower and
 a gem.
And love, like a flower, will fade, will change into something
 else
or it would not be flowery.

O flowers they fade because they are moving swiftly; a little
 torrent of life
leaps up to the summit of the stem, gleams, turns over round
 the bend
of the parabola of curved flight,
sinks, and is gone, like a comet curving into the invisible.

O flowers they are all the time travelling
like comets, and they come into our ken
for a day, for two days, and withdraw, slowly vanish again.

And we, we must take them on the wing, and let them go.
Embalmed flowers are not flowers, immortelles are not flowers;
flowers are just a motion, a swift motion, a coloured gesture;
that is their loveliness. And that is love.

But a gem is different. It lasts so much longer than we do
so much much much longer
that it seems to last forever.
Yet we know it is flowing away
as flowers are, and we are, only slower.
The wonderful slow flowing of the sapphire!

All flows, and every flow is related to every other flow.
Flowers and sapphires and us, diversely streaming.

In the old days, when sapphires were breathed upon and
    brought forth
during the wild orgasms of chaos
time was much slower, when the rocks came forth.
It took æons to make a sapphire, æons for it to pass away.

And a flower it takes a summer.

And man and woman are like the earth, that brings forth
    flowers
in summer, and love, but underneath is rock.
Older than flowers, older than ferns, older than foraminiferæ
older than plasm altogether is the soul of a man underneath.

And when, throughout all the wild orgasms of love
slowly a gem forms, in the ancient, once-more-molten rocks
of two human hearts, two ancient rocks, a man's heart and a
    woman's,
that is the crystal of peace, the slow hard jewel of trust,
the sapphire of fidelity.
The gem of mutual peace emerging from the wild chaos of love.

KNOW DEEPLY, KNOW THYSELF MORE DEEPLY——

Go deeper than love, for the soul has greater depths,
love is like the grass, but the heart is deep wild rock
molten, yet dense and permanent.

Go down to your deep old heart, woman, and lose sight of
    yourself.
And lose sight of me, the me whom you turbulently loved.

Let us lose sight of ourselves, and break the mirrors.
For the fierce curve of our lives is moving again to the depths
out of sight, in the deep dark living heart.

But say, in the dark wild metal of your heart
is there a gem, which came into being between us?
is there a sapphire of mutual trust, a blue spark?
Is there a ruby of fused being, mine and yours, an inward glint?

If there is not, O then leave me, go away.
For I cannot be bullied back into the appearances of love,
any more than August can be bullied to look like March.

Love out of season, especially at the end of the season
is merely ridiculous.
If you insist on it, I insist on departure.

Have you no deep old heart of wild womanhood
self-forgetful, and gemmed with experience,
and swinging in a strange unison of power
with the heart of the man you are supposed to have loved?

If you have not, go away.
If you can only sit with a mirror in your hand, an ageing
    woman
posing on and on as a lover,
in love with a self that now is shallow and withered,
your own self—that has passed like a last summer's flower—
then go away—

I do not want a woman whom age cannot wither.
She is a made-up lie, a dyed immortelle
of infinite staleness.

ALL I ASK——

ALL I ask of a woman is that she shall feel gently towards me
when my heart feels kindly towards her,
and there shall be the soft, soft tremor as of unheard bells
 between us.
It is all I ask.
I am so tired of violent women lashing out and insisting
on being loved, when there is no love in them.

THE UNIVERSE FLOWS——

THE universe flows in infinite wild streams, related
in rhythms too big and too small for us to know,
since man is just middling, and his comprehension just
 middling.

If once, for a second, the universe ceased to flow
of course it would cease to exist.
The thought is unthinkable, anyhow.

Only man tries not to flow,
repeats himself over and over in mechanical monotony of conceit
and hence is a mess.

If only Cleopatra had left off being so Cleopatra-ish
—she was it too long—
if only she had gone down to a deeper self in herself
as time went on,
Anthony might have made a splendid thing of the East,
she might have saved herself the asp
and him from sticking himself like a pig
and us from the dreary inheritance of Roman stupidity.

UNDERNEATH——

BELOW what we think we are
we are something else,
we are almost anything.

Below the grass and trees
and streets and houses and even seas
is rock; and below the rock, the rock
is we know not what,
the hot wild core of the earth, heavier than we can even imagine.

Pivotal core of the soul, heavier than iron
so ponderously central;
heavier and hotter than anything known;
and also alone.—
And yet
reeling with connection
spinning with the heaviness of balance
and flowing invisibly, gasping
towards the breathing stars and the central of all sunninesses.

The earth leans its weight on the sun, and the sun on the sun of suns.
Back and forth goes the balance and the electric breath.

The soul of man also leans in the unconscious inclination we call religion
towards the sun of suns, and back and forth goes the breath
of incipient energetic life.

Out of the soul's middle to the middle-most sun, way-off, or in every atom.

THE PRIMAL PASSIONS

If you will go down into yourself, under your surface personality
you will find you have a great desire to drink life direct
from the source, not out of bottles and bottled personal vessels

What the old people call immediate contact with God.
That strange essential communication of life
not bottled in human bottles.

What even the wild witchcraft of the past was seeking
before it degenerated.

Life from the source, unadulterated
with the human taint.

Contact with the sun of suns
that shines somewhere in the atom, somewhere pivots the curved space,
and cares not a straw for the put-up human figments.

Communion with the Godhead, they used to say in the past.
But even that is human-tainted now,
tainted with the ego and the personality.

To feel a fine, fine breeze blowing through the navel and the knees
and have a cool sense of truth, inhuman truth at last
softly fluttering the senses, in the exquisite orgasm of coition
with the godhead of energy that cannot tell lies.

The cool, cool truth of pure vitality
pouring into the veins from the direct contact with the source.
Uncontaminated by even the beginnings of a lie.

The soul's first passion is for sheer life
entering in shocks of truth, unfouled by lies.

And the soul's next passion is to reflect
and then turn round and embrace the extant body of life
with the thrusting embrace of new justice, new justice
between men and men, men and women, and earth and stars,
    and suns.
The passion of justice being profound and subtle
and changing in a flow as all passions change.

But the passion of justice is a primal embrace
between man and all his known universe.

And the passion of truth is the embrace between man and his
    god
in the sheer coition of the life-flow, stark and unlying.

ESCAPE

WHEN we get out of the glass bottles of our own ego,
and when we escape like squirrels from turning in the cages
    of our personality
and get into the forest again,
we shall shiver with cold and fright
but things will happen to us
so that we don't know ourselves.

Cool, unlying life will rush in,
and passion will make our bodies taut with power,
we shall stamp our feet with new power
and old things will fall down,
we shall laugh, and institutions will curl up like burnt paper.

THE ROOT OF OUR EVIL——

The root of our present evil is that we buy and sell.
Ultimately, we are all busy buying and selling one another.

It began with Judas, and goes on in the wage-system.
Men sell themselves for a wage, and employers look out for a bargain.
And employers are bought by financiers, and financiers are sold to the devil.

—Get thou behind me, Satan!—
That was just what Satan wanted to do,
for then nobody would have their eye on him.

And Jesus never looked round.
That is the great reproach we have against *him*.
He was frightened to look round
and see Satan bargaining the world away
and men, and the bread of men
behind his back
with satanically inspired financiers.

If Jesus had kept a sharp eye on Satan,
and refused to let so many things happen behind his back
we shouldn't be where we are now.

Come, Satan, don't go dodging behind my back any longer.
If you've got the goods, come forward, boy, and let's see 'em.
I'm perfectly willing to strike a decent bargain.
But I'm not having any dodging going on behind my back.—

What we want is some sort of communism
not based on wages, nor profits, nor any sort of buying and
    selling
but on a religion of life.

THE IGNOBLE PROCESSION

When I see the ignoble procession
streaming forth from little doorways
citywards, in little rivers that swell to a great stream,
of men in bowler hats, hurrying
and a mingling of wallet-carrying women
hurrying, hurrying, legs going quick quick quick
in ignoble haste, for fear of being late—
I am filled with humiliation.

Their haste
is so
humiliating.

NO JOY IN LIFE

Never, my young men,
you who complain you know no joy in your lives,
never will you know any joy in your lives
till you ask for lightning instead of love
till you pray to the right gods, for the thunder-bolt instead of
    pity
till you look to the right man, to put you into touch.

Then you will hit the Flat-iron Building and flatten it out.
Then you will shatter the Bank.
Then you will settle the hash of Business finally.

WILD THINGS IN CAPTIVITY

WILD things in captivity
while they keep their own wild purity
won't breed, they mope, they die.

All men are in captivity,
active with captive activity,
and the best won't breed, though they don't know why.

The great cage of our domesticity
kills sex in a man, the simplicity
of desire is distorted and twisted awry.

And so, with bitter perversity,
gritting against the great adversity,
the young ones copulate, hate it, and want to cry.

Sex is a state of grace.
In a cage it can't take place.
Break the cage then, start in and try.

MOURNFUL YOUNG MAN——

MOURNFUL young man in your twenties
who think the only way out of your mournfulness is through
    a woman,
yet you fail to find the woman, when there are so many women
    about—

Why don't you realise
that you're not desirable?
that no woman will ever desire you, as you are,
except, of course, for secondary motives.

The women are in the cage as much as you are.
They look at you, they see a caged monkey.
How do you expect them ever to desire you?
Anyhow they never will, except for secondary motives,
or except you change.

MONEY-MADNESS

MONEY is our madness, our vast collective madness.

And of course, if the multitude is mad
the individual carries his own grain of insanity around with
    him.

I doubt if any man living hands out a pound note without a
    pang;
and a real tremor, if he hands out a ten-pound note.

We quail, money makes us quail.
It has got us down, we grovel before it in strange terror.
And no wonder, for money has a fearful cruel power among
    men.

But it is not money we are so terrified of,
it is the collective money-madness of mankind.
For mankind says with one voice: How much is he worth?
Has he no money? Then let him eat dirt, and go cold.—

And if I have no money, they will give me a little bread
so I do not die,
but they will make me eat dirt with it.
I shall have to eat dirt, I shall have to eat dirt
if I have no money.

It is that that I am frightened of.
And that fear can become a delirium.
It is fear of my money-mad fellow-men.

We must have some money
to save us from eating dirt.

And this is all wrong.

Bread should be free,
shelter should be free,
fire should be free
to all and anybody, all and anybody, all over the world.

We must regain our sanity about money
before we start killing one another about it.
It's one thing or the other.

KILL MONEY——

KILL money, put money out of existence.
It is a perverted instinct, a hidden thought
which rots the brain, the blood, the bones, the stones, the soul.

Make up your mind about it:
that society must establish itself upon a different principle
from the one we've got now.

We must have the courage of mutual trust.
We must have the modesty of simple living.
And the individual must have his house, food and fire all free
like a bird.

MEN ARE NOT BAD——

MEN are not bad, when they are free.
Prison makes men bad, and the money compulsion makes men
    bad.
If men were free from the terror of earning a living
there would be abundance in the world
and men would work gaily.

NOTTINGHAM'S NEW UNIVERSITY

IN Nottingham, that dismal town
where I went to school and college,
they've built a new university
for a new dispensation of knowledge.

Built it most grand and cakeily
out of the noble loot
derived from shrewd cash-chemistry
by good Sir Jesse Boot.

Little I thought, when I was a lad
and turned my modest penny
over on Boot's Cash Chemist's counter,
that Jesse, by turning many

millions of similar honest pence
over, would make a pile
that would rise at last and blossom out
in grand and cakey style

into a university
where smart men would dispense
doses of smart cash-chemistry
in language of common-sense!

That future Nottingham lads would be
cash-chemically B.Sc.
that Nottingham lights would rise and say:
—By Boots I am M.A.

From this I learn, though I knew it before
that culture has her roots
in the deep dung of cash, and lore
is a last offshoot of Boots.

I AM IN A NOVEL——

I READ a novel by a friend of mine
in which one of the characters was me,
the novel it sure was mighty fine
but the funniest thing that could be

was me, or what was supposed for me,
for I had to recognise
a few of the touches, like a low-born jake,
but the rest was a real surprise.

Well damn my eyes! I said to myself.
Well damn my little eyes!
If this is what Archibald thinks I am
he sure thinks a lot of lies.

Well think o' that now, think o' that!
That's what he sees in me!
I'm about as much like a Persian cat,
or a dog with a harrowing flea.

My Lord! a man's friends' ideas of him
would stock a menagerie
with a marvellous outfit! How did Archie see
such a funny pup in me?

NO! MR LAWRENCE!

No, Mr Lawrence, it's not like that!
I don't mind telling you
I know a thing or two about love,
perhaps more than you do.

And what I know is that you make it
too nice, too beautiful.
It's not like that, you know; you fake it.
It's really rather dull.

RED-HERRING

My father was a working man
    and a collier was he,
at six in the morning they turned him down
    and they turned him up for tea.

My mother was a superior soul
    a superior soul was she,
cut out to play a superior rôle
    in the god-damn bourgeoisie.

We children were the in-betweens
　　little non-descripts were we,
indoors we called each other *you*,
　　outside, it was *tha* and *thee*.

But time has fled, our parents are dead
　　we've risen in the world all three;
but still we are in-betweens, we tread
　　between the devil and the deep cold sea.

O I am a member of the bourgeoisie
　　and a servant-maid brings me my tea—
But I'm always longing for someone to say:
　　'ark 'ere, lad! atween thee an' me

they're a' a b—d— lot o' ——s,
　　an' I reckon it's nowt but right
we should start an' kick their ——ses for 'em
　　an' tell 'em to ——.

OUR MORAL AGE

Of course, if you make naughtiness nasty,
　　　spicily nasty, of course,
then it's quite all right; we understand
　　　life's voice, even when she's hoarse.

But if you go and make naughtiness nice
　　　there's no excuse;
if such things were nice, and we needn't think twice
　　　what would be the use—?

WHEN I READ SHAKESPEARE——

When I read Shakespeare I am struck with wonder
that such trivial people should muse and thunder
in such lovely language.

Lear, the old buffer, you wonder his daughters
didn't treat him rougher,
the old chough, the old chuffer!

And Hamlet, how boring, how boring to live with,
so mean and self-conscious, blowing and snoring
his wonderful speeches, full of other folks' whoring!

And Macbeth and his Lady, who should have been choring,
such suburban ambition, so messily goring
old Duncan with daggers!

How boring, how small Shakespeare's people are!
Yet the language so lovely! like the dyes from gas-tar.

SALT OF THE EARTH

Slowly the salt of the earth becomes salt of the sea.
Slowly the raindrops of appreciation
carry the salt of the earth, the wisdom of wise men, the gifts
    of the great
down to the ocean of the afterwards, where it remains as brine
in which to pickle the younger generations
who would be so much better without pickling.

Slowly the salt of the earth becomes salt of the sea.

FRESH WATER

They say it is very difficult
to distil sea-water into sweet.

Perhaps that's why it is so difficult
to get a refreshing drink out of old wisdom
old truth, old teaching of any sort.

PEACE AND WAR

People always make war when they say they love peace.
The loud love of peace makes one quiver more than any battle-cry.
Why should one love peace? it is so obviously vile to make war.
Loud peace propaganda makes war seem imminent.
It is a form of war, even, self-assertion and being wise for other people.
Let people be wise for themselves. And anyhow
nobody can be wise except on rare occasions, like getting married or dying.
It's bad taste to be wise all the time, like being at a perpetual funeral.
For everyday use, give me somebody whimsical, with not too much purpose in life,
then we shan't have war, and we needn't talk about peace.

MANY MANSIONS

When a bird flips his tail in getting his balance on a tree
he feels much gayer than if somebody had left him a fortune
or than if he'd just built himself a nest with a bathroom—
Why can't people be gay like that?

GLORY

Glory is of the sun, too, and the sun of suns,
and down the shafts of his splendid pinions
run tiny rivers of peace.

Most of his time, the tiger pads and slouches in a burning
    peace.
And the small hawk high up turns round on the slow pivot of
    peace.
Peace comes from behind the sun, with the peregrine falcon,
    and the owl.
Yet all of these drink blood.—

WOE

Woe, woe to the world!
For we're all self-consciously aware of ourselves
yet not sufficiently conscious to be able to forget ourselves
and be whimsically at home in ourselves.

So everybody makes an assertion of himself,
and every self-assertion clashes on every other.

ATTILA

I would call Attila on his little horse
a man of peace.

For after all, he helped to smash a lot of old Roman lies,
the lies, the treachery, the slippery cultured squalor of that
    sneaking court of Ravenna.

And after all, lying and base hypocrisy and treachery
are much more hellishly peaceless than a little straightforward
    bloodshed
which may occasionally be a preliminary to the peace that
    passes understanding.

So that I would call Attila on his little horse
a man of peace.

WHAT WOULD YOU FIGHT FOR?

I AM not sure I would always fight for my life.
Life might not be worth fighting for.

I am not sure I would always fight for my wife.
A wife isn't always worth fighting for.

Nor my children, nor my country, nor my fellow-men.
It all depends whether I found them worth fighting for.

The only thing men invariably fight for
is their money. But I doubt if I'd fight for mine, anyhow not
    to shed a lot of blood over it.

Yet one thing I do fight for, tooth and nail, all the time.
And that is my bit of inward peace, where I am at one with
    myself.

And I must say, I am often worsted.

CHOICE

I WOULD rather sit still in a state of peace on a stone
than ride in the motor-car of a multimillionaire
and feel the peacelessness of the multimillionaire
poisoning me.

RICHES

When I wish I was rich, then I know I am ill.
Because, to tell the truth, I have enough as I am.
So when I catch myself thinking: Ah, if I was rich—!
I say to myself: Hello! I'm not well. My vitality is low.

POVERTY

The only people I ever heard talk about My Lady Poverty
were rich people, or people who imagined themselves rich.
Saint Francis himself was a rich and spoiled young man.

Being born among the working people
I know that poverty is a hard old hag,
and a monster, when you're pinched for actual necessities.
And whoever says she isn't, is a liar.

I don't want to be poor, it means I am pinched.
But neither do I want to be rich.
When I look at this pine-tree near the sea,
that grows out of rock, and plumes forth, plumes forth,
I see it has a natural abundance.

With its roots it has a grand grip on its daily bread,
and its plumes look like green cups held up to sun and air
and full of wine.

I want to be like that, to have a natural abundance
and plume forth, and be splendid.

NOBLE

I know I am noble with the nobility of the sun.
A certain peace, a certain grace.
I would say the same if I were a chaffinch or tree.

WEALTH

PEACE I have from the core of the atom, from the core of space,
and grace, if I don't lose it, from the same place.
And I look shabby, yet my roots go beyond my knowing,
deep beyond the world of man.
And where my little leaves flutter highest
there are no people, nor ever will be.

Yet my roots are in a woman too.
And my leaves are green with the breath of human experience.

TOLERANCE

ONE can be tolerant with a bore
and suffer fools, though not gladly
—why should a man pretend to be glad about his sufferings?—

But it is hard to be tolerant with the smarties,
or to put up with the clever mess-makers,
or to endure the jazzy person;
one can't stand peaceless people any more.

COMPARI

I WOULD like a few men to be at peace with.
Not friends, necessarily, they talk so much.
Nor yet comrades, for I don't belong to any cause.
Nor yet " brothers," it's so conceited.
Nor pals, they're such a nuisance.
But men to be at peace with.

SICK

I am sick, because I have given myself away.
I have given myself to the people when they came
so cultured, even bringing little gifts,
so they pecked a shred of my life, and flew off with a croak
of sneaking exultance.
So now I have lost too much, and am sick.

I am trying now to learn never
to give of my life to the dead,
never, not the tiniest shred.

DEAD PEOPLE

When people are dead and peaceless
they hate life, they only like carrion.

When people are dead and peaceless
they hate happiness in others
with thin, screaming hatred,
as the vulture that screams high up, almost inaudible,
hovering to peck out the eyes of the still-living creature.

CEREBRAL EMOTIONS

I am sick of people's cerebral emotions
that are born in their minds and forced down by the will
on to their poor deranged bodies.

People feeling things they intend to feel, they mean to feel,
they *will* feel,
just because they don't feel them.

For of course, if you really feel something
you don't have to assert that you feel it.

WELLSIAN FUTURES

When men are made in bottles
and emerge as squeaky globules with no bodies to speak of,
and therefore nothing to have feelings with,

they will still squeak intensely about their feelings
and be prepared to kill you if you say they've got none.

TO WOMEN, AS FAR AS I'M CONCERNED

The feelings I don't have I don't have.
The feelings I don't have, I won't say I have.
The feelings you say you have, you don't have.
The feelings you would like us both to have, we neither of us
    have.
The feelings people ought to have, they never have.
If people say they've got feelings, you may be pretty sure they
    haven't got them.

So if you want either of us to feel anything at all
you'd better abandon all idea of feelings altogether.

BLANK

At present I am a blank, and I admit it.
In feeling I am just a blank.
My mind is fairly nimble, and is not blank.
My body likes its dinner and the warm sun, but otherwise is
    blank.
My soul is almost blank, my spirit quite.
I have a certain amount of money, so my anxieties are blank.

And I can't do anything about it, even there I am blank.
So I am just going to go on being a blank, till something
    nudges me from within,
and makes me know I am not blank any longer.

ELDERLY DISCONTENTED WOMEN

ELDERLY discontented women ask for intimate companionship,
by which they mean more talk, talk, talk
especially about themselves and their own feelings.

Elderly discontented women are so full of themselves
they have high blood-pressure and almost burst.

It is as if modern women had all got themselves on the brain
and that sent the blood rushing to the surface of the body
and driving them around in frenzied energy
stampeding over everybody,
while their hearts become absolutely empty,
and their voices are like screw-drivers
as they try to screw everybody else down with their will.

OLD PEOPLE

NOWADAYS everybody wants to be young,
so much so, that even the young are old with the effort of
    being young.
As for those over fifty, either they rush forward in self-assertion
fearful to behold,
or they bear everybody a grim and grisly grudge
because of their own fifty or sixty or seventy or eighty summers.
As if it's my fault that the old girl is seventy-seven!

THE GRUDGE OF THE OLD

The old ones want to be young, and they aren't young,
and it rankles, they ache when they see the young,
and they can't help wanting to spite it on them
venomously.

The old ones say to themselves: We are not going to be old,
we are not going to make way, we are not going to die,
we are going to stay on and on and on and on and on
and make the young look after us
till they are old. We are stronger than the young.
We have more energy, and our grip on life is harder.
Let us triumph, and let the young be listless
with their puny youth.
We are younger even now than the young, we can put their
    youth in abeyance.

And it is true.
And they do it.
And so it goes on.

BEAUTIFUL OLD AGE

It ought to be lovely to be old
to be full of the peace that comes of experience
and wrinkled ripe fulfilment.

The wrinkled smile of completeness that follows a life
lived undaunted and unsoured with accepted lies.
If people lived without accepting lies
they would ripen like apples, and be scented like pippins
in their old age.

Soothing, old people should be, like apples
when one is tired of love.
Fragrant like yellowing leaves, and dim with the soft
stillness and satisfaction of autumn.

And a girl should say :
It must be wonderful to live and grow old.
Look at my mother, how rich and still she is !—

And a young man should think : By Jove
my father has faced all weathers, but it's been a life !—

COURAGE

WHAT makes people unsatisfied
is that they accept lies.

If people had courage, and refused lies
and found out what they really felt and really meant
and acted on it,

they would distil the essential oil out of every experience
and like hazel-nuts in autumn, at last
be sweet and sound.

And the young among the old
would be as in the hazel-woods of September
nutting, gathering nuts of ripe experience.

As it is, all that the old can offer
is sour, bitter fruits, cankered by lies.

DESIRE IS DEAD

Desire may be dead
and still a man can be
a meeting place for sun and rain,
wonder outwaiting pain
as in a wintry tree.

WHEN THE RIPE FRUIT FALLS——

When the ripe fruit falls
its sweetness distils and trickles away into the veins of the earth

When fulfilled people die
the essential oil of their experience enters
the veins of living space, and adds a glisten
to the atom, to the body of immortal chaos.

For space is alive
and it stirs like a swan
whose feathers glisten
silky with oil of distilled experience.

ELEMENTAL

Why don't people leave off being lovable
or thinking they are lovable, or wanting to be lovable,
and be a bit elemental instead?

Since man is made up of the elements
fire, and rain, and air, and live loam
and none of these is lovable
but elemental,
man is lop-sided on the side of the angels.

I wish men would get back their balance among the elements
and be a bit more fiery, as incapable of telling lies
as fire is.
I wish they'd be true to their own variation, as water is,
which goes through all the stages of steam and stream and ice
without losing its head.

I am sick of lovable people,
somehow they are a lie.

FIRE

FIRE is dearer to us than love or food,
hot, hurrying, yet it burns if you touch it.

What we ought to do
is not to add our love together, or our good-will, or any of that,
for we're sure to bring in a lot of lies,
but our fire, our elemental fire
so that it rushes up in a huge blaze like a phallus into hollow
    space
and fecundates the zenith and the nadir
and sends off millions of sparks of new atoms
and singes us, and burns the house down.

I WISH I KNEW A WOMAN—

I WISH I knew a woman
who was like a red fire on the hearth
glowing after the day's restless draughts.

So that one could draw near her
in the red stillness of the dusk
and really take delight in her

without having to make the polite effort of loving her
or the mental effort of making her acquaintance.
Without having to take a chill, talking to her.

TALK

I wish people, when you sit near them,
wouldn't think it necessary to make conversation
and send thin draughts of words
blowing down your neck and your ears
and giving you a cold in your inside.

THE EFFORT OF LOVE

I am worn out
with the effort of trying to love people
and not succeeding.

Now I've made up my mind
I love nobody, I'm going to love nobody,
I'm not going to tell any lies about it
and it's final.

If there's a man here and there, or a woman
whom I can really like,
that's quite enough for me.

And if by a miracle a woman happened to come along
who warmed the cockles of my heart
I'd rejoice over the woman and the warmed cockles of my
    heart
so long as it didn't all fizzle out in talk.

CAN'T BE BORNE——

ANY woman who says to me
—Do you really love me?—
earns my undying detestation.

MAN REACHES A POINT——

I CANNOT help but be alone
for desire has died in me, silence has grown,
and nothing now reaches out to draw
other flesh to my own.

GRASSHOPPER IS A BURDEN——

DESIRE has failed, desire has failed
and the critical grasshopper
has come down on the heart in a burden of locusts
and stripped it bare.

BASTA!

WHEN a man can love no more
and feel no more
and desire has failed
and the heart is numb

then all he can do
is to say: It is so!
I've got to put up with it
and wait.
This is a pause, how long a pause I know not,
in my very being.

TRAGEDY

TRAGEDY seems to me a loud noise
louder than is seemly.

Tragedy looks to me like man
in love with his own defeat.
Which is only a sloppy way of being in love with yourself.

I can't very much care about the woes and tragedies
of Lear and Macbeth and Hamlet and Timon:
they cared so excessively themselves.

And when I think of the great tragedy of our material-
    mechanical civilisation
crushing out the natural human life
then sometimes I feel defeated; and then again I know
my shabby little defeat would do neither me any good
nor anybody else.

AFTER ALL THE TRAGEDIES ARE OVER——

AFTER all the tragedies are over and worn out
and a man can no longer feel heroic about being a Hamlet—

When love is gone, and desire is dead, and tragedy has left
    the heart
then grief and pain go too, withdrawing
from the heart and leaving strange cold stretches of sand.

So a man no longer knows his own heart;
he might say into the twilight: What is it?
I am here, yet my heart is bare and utterly empty.
I have passed from existence, I feel nothing any more.
I am a nonentity.—

Yet, when the time has come to be nothing, how good it is to
> be nothing!
a waste expanse of nothing, like wide foreshores where not a
> ripple is left
and the sea is lost
in the lapse of the lowest of tides.

Ah, when I have seen myself left by life, left nothing!

Yet even waste, grey foreshores, sand, and sorry, far-out clay
are sea-bed still, through their hour of bare denuding.
It is the moon that turns the tides.
The beaches can do nothing about it.

NULLUS

I know I am nothing.
Life has gone away, below my low-water mark.

I am aware I feel nothing, even at dawn.
The dawn comes up with a glitter and a blueness, and I say:
> How lovely!—
But I am a liar, I feel no loveliness, it is a mental remark, a
> cliché.

My whole consciousness is cliché
and I am null;
I exist as an organism
and a nullus.

But I can do nothing about it
except admit it and leave it to the moon.

There are said to be creative pauses,
pauses that are as good as death, empty and dead as death itself.
And in these awful pauses the evolutionary change takes place.
Perhaps it is so.
The tragedy is over, it has ceased to be tragic, the last pause
    is upon us.
Pause, brethren, pause!

DIES IRAE

EVEN the old emotions are finished,
we have worn them out.
And desire is dead.
And the end of all things is inside us.

Our epoch is over,
a cycle of evolution is finished,
our activity has lost its meaning,
we are ghosts, we are seed;
for our word is dead
and we know not how to live wordless.

We live in a vast house
full of inordinate activities,
and the noise, and the stench, and the dreariness and lack of
    meaning
madden us, but we don't know what to do.

All we can know at this moment
is the fulfilment of nothingness.
Lo, I am nothing!

It is a consummation devoutly to be wished
in this world of mechanical self-assertion.

DIES ILLA

Dies irae, dies illa
solvet saeclum in favilla—

Day of wrath, O day of warning!
Flame devours the world.

It does, even if we don't see it.
For there are all sorts of flame:
slow, creeping cold ones
that burn inwardly
like flickering cancers.

And the slow cold flames
may burn for long years
before they've eaten through the joists and the girders
and the house comes down, with a subsiding crash.

STOP IT——

The one thing the old will never understand
is that you can't prevent change.
All flows, and even the old are rapidly flowing away.
And the young are flowing in the throes of a great alteration

THE DEATH OF OUR ERA

Our era is dying
yet who has killed it?
Have we, who are it?

In the middle of voluted space
its knell has struck.
And in the middle of every atom, which is the same thing,
a tiny bell of conclusion has sounded.

The curfew of our great day
the passing-bell of our way of knowing
the knell of our bald-headed consciousness
the tocsin of this our civilisation.

Who struck the bell?
Who rang the knell?
Not I, not you,
yet all of us.

At the core of space the final knell
of our era has struck, and it chimes
in terrible rippling circles between the stars
till it reaches us, and its vibrations shatter us
each time they touch us.

And they keep on coming, with greater force
striking us, the vibrations of our finish.

And all that we can do
is to die the amazing death
with every stroke, and go on
till we are blank.

And yet, as we die, why should not our vast mechanised day
    die with us,
so that when we are re-born, we can be born into a fresh world.

For the new word is Resurrection.

THE NEW WORD

SHALL I tell you again the new word,
the new word of the unborn day?
It is Resurrection.
The resurrection of the flesh.

For our flesh is dead
only egoistically we assert ourselves.

And the new word means nothing to us,
it is such an old word,
till we admit how dead we are,
till we actually feel as blank as we really are.

SUN IN ME

A sun will rise in me,
I shall slowly resurrect,
already the whiteness of false dawn is on my inner ocean.

A sun in me.
And a sun in heaven.
And beyond that, the immense sun behind the sun,
the sun of immense distances, that fold themselves together
within the genitals of living space.
And further, the sun within the atom
which is god in the atom.

BE STILL!

THE only thing to be done, now,
now that the waves of our undoing have begun to strike on us
is to contain ourselves.

To keep still, and let the wreckage of ourselves go,
let everything go, as the wave smashes us,
yet keep still, and hold
the tiny grain of something that no wave can wash away
not even the most massive wave of destiny.

Among all the smashed debris of myself
keep quiet, and wait.
For the word is Resurrection.
And even the sea of seas will have to give up its dead.

AT LAST——

When things get very bad, they pass beyond tragedy.
And then the only thing we can do is to keep quite still
and guard the last treasure of the soul, our sanity.

Since, poor individuals that we are,
if we lose our sanity
we lose that which keeps us individual
distinct from chaos.

In death, the atom takes us up
and the suns.
But if we lose our sanity
nothing and nobody in the whole vast realm of space
wants us, or can have anything to do with us.
We can but howl the lugubrious howl of idiots,
the howl of the utterly lost
howling their nowhereness.

NEMESIS

The Nemesis that awaits our civilisation
is social insanity
which in the end is always homicidal.

Sanity means the wholeness of the consciousness.
And our society is only part conscious, like an idiot.

If we do not rapidly open all the doors of consciousness
and freshen the putrid little space in which we are cribbed
the sky-blue walls of our unventilated heaven
will be bright red with blood.

THE OPTIMIST

The optimist builds himself safe inside a cell
and paints the inside walls sky-blue
and blocks up the door
and says he's in heaven.

THE THIRD THING

Water is H_2O, hydrogen two parts, oxygen one,
but there is also a third thing, that makes it water
and nobody knows what that is.

The atom locks up two energies
but it is a third thing present which makes it an atom.

THE SANE UNIVERSE

One might talk of the sanity of the atom,
the sanity of space,
the sanity of the electron,
the sanity of water—

For it is all alive
and has something comparable to that which we call sanity
    in ourselves.
The only oneness is the oneness of sanity.

FEAR OF SOCIETY IS THE ROOT OF ALL EVIL

To-day, the social consciousness is mutilated
so everything is insane:
success is insane, and failure is insane,
chastity is insane, and debauchery is insane,
money is insane, and poverty is insane.

A fearful thing is the mutilated social consciousness.

GOD

Where sanity is
there God is.
And the sane can still recognise sanity
so they can still recognise God.

SANE AND INSANE

The puritan is insane
and the profligate is insane
and they divide the world.

The wealthy are insane
and the poverty-stricken are insane
and the world is going to pieces between them.

The puritan is afraid
and the profligate is afraid.

The wealthy are afraid
and the poverty-stricken are afraid.

They are afraid with horrible and opposing fears
which threaten to tear the world in two, between them.

A SANE REVOLUTION

If you make a revolution, make it for fun,
don't make it in ghastly seriousness,
don't do it in deadly earnest,
do it for fun.

Don't do it because you hate people,
do it just to spit in their eye.

Don't do it for the money,
do it and be damned to the money.

Don't do it for equality,
do it because we've got too much equality
and it would be fun to upset the apple-cart
and see which way the apples would go a-rolling.

Don't do it for the working classes.
Do it so that we can all of us be little aristocracies on our own
and kick our heels like jolly escaped asses.

Don't do it, anyhow, for international Labour.
Labour is the one thing a man has had too much of.
Let's abolish labour, let's have done with labouring!
Work can be fun, and men can enjoy it; then it's not labour.
Let's have it so! Let's make a revolution for fun!

ALWAYS THIS PAYING

Nothing is really any fun, to-day,
because you've always got to pay for everything.
And whatever costs you money, money, money, is really no
    fun.

That's why women aren't much fun. You're always having
    to pay for them.
Or else, poor things, they're having to pay for themselves,
which is perhaps worse.
Why isn't anything free, why is it always pay, pay, pay?

A man can't get any fun out of wife, sweetheart or tart
because of the beastly expense.

Why don't we do something about the money system?

POOR YOUNG THINGS

The young to-day are born prisoners,
poor things, and they know it.
Born in a universal workhouse,
and they feel it.
Inheriting a sort of confinement,
work, and prisoners' routine
and prisoners' flat, ineffectual pastime.

A PLAYED-OUT GAME

Success is a played-out game, success, success!
because what have you got when you've got it?

The young aren't vitally interested in it any more.
Only third-rate swabs are pushing to get on, nowadays.

Getting the better of other people! Who cares?—
Getting the better of them! Which better, what better, anyhow?

Our poor old daddies *got on*,
and then could never get off again.

If only we could make life a bit more just
so that we could all get along gaily
instead of getting on and not being able to get off again.

TRIUMPH

IT seems to me that for five thousand years at least
men have been wanting to triumph, triumph, triumph,
triumph over their fellow-men, triumph over obstacles, triumph
    over evil,
till now the very word is nauseating, we can't hear it any
    more.

If we looked in our hearts we should see
we loathe the thought of any sort of triumph,
we are sick of it.

THE COMBATIVE SPIRIT

As a matter of fact, we are better than we know.
We trail behind us an endless tradition, of combat, triumph,
    conquest,
and we feel we've got to keep it up, keep on combating,
    triumphing, conquering.

When as a matter of fact, the thought of this endless, imbecile
    struggle of combat
kills us, we are sick of it to die.
We are fed up with combat,
we feel that if the whole combative, competitive system
    doesn't soon go bust
we shall.
We want a new world of wild peace, where living is free.

Not this hyena tame peace where no man dare tell another
    he's a thief
and yet every man is driven into robbing every other man;
this pretty peace where every man has to fight, and fight foul,
to get a living, in the dastardly mean combat
we call free competition and individual enterprise and equal
    opportunity.

Why should we have to fight for a living?
Living should be as free to a man as to a bird,
though most birds have to pay, with their lives, where men
    are.

Why should we brace ourselves up with mean emulation?
If we brace ourselves up, it should be for something we want
    to do
and we feel is worth doing.
The efforts of men, like the efforts of birds in spring,
would be lovely if they rose from the man himself, spontaneous
pure impulse to make something, to put something forth.
Even if it was only a tin pan.

I see the tin-man, the tinker, sitting day after day on the beach
mending and tinning the pans of all the village
and happy as a wagtail by a pool,
the same with the fishermen sitting darning their nets,
happy as perhaps kings used to be, but certainly aren't.
Work is the clue to a man's life.
But it must be free work, not done just for money, but for fun.

Why should we compete with one another?
As a matter of fact, when the tinker looks so happy tinkering
I immediately want to go and do something jolly too.
One free, cheerful activity stimulates another.
Men are not really mean.
Men are made mean, by fear, and a system of grab.

The young know these things quite well.
Why don't they prepare to act on them?
Then they'd be happy. For we are all so much better than the system allows us to be.

WAGES

The wages of work is cash.
The wages of cash is want more cash.
The wages of want more cash is vicious competition.
The wages of vicious competition is—the world we live in.

The work-cash-want circle is the viciousest circle
that ever turned men into fiends.

Earning a wage is a prison occupation
and a wage-earner is a sort of gaol-bird.

112

Earning a salary is a prison overseer's job,
a gaoler instead of a gaol-bird.

Living on your income is strolling grandly outside the prison
in terror lest you have to go in. And since the work-prison covers
almost every scrap of the living earth, you stroll up and down
on a narrow beat, about the same as a prisoner taking his exercise.

This is called universal freedom.

YOUNG FATHERS

Young men, having no real joy in life and no hope in the future
how can they commit the indecency of begetting children
without first begetting a new hope for the children to grow
up to?

But then, you need only look at the modern perambulator
to see that a child, as soon as it is born,
is put by its parents into its coffin.

A TALE TOLD BY AN IDIOT

Modern life is a tale told by an idiot;
flat-chested, crop-headed, chemicalised women, of indeterminate sex,
and wimbly-wambly young men, of sex still more indeterminate,
and hygienic babies in huge hulks of coffin-like perambulators—

The great social idiot, it must be confessed,
tells dull, meaningless, disgusting tales,
and repeats himself like the flushing of a W.C.

BEING ALIVE

The only reason for living is being fully alive;
and you can't be fully alive if you are crushed by secret fear,
and bullied with the threat: Get money, or eat dirt!—
and forced to do a thousand mean things meaner than your
    nature,
and forced to clutch on to possessions in the hope they'll make
    you feel safe,
and forced to watch everyone that comes near you, lest they've
    come to do you down.

Without a bit of common trust in one another, we can't live.
In the end, we go insane.
It is the penalty of fear and meanness, being meaner than our
    natures are.

To be alive, you've got to feel a generous flow,
and under a competitive system that is impossible, really.
The world is waiting for a new great movement of generosity,
or for a great wave of death.
We must change the system, and make living free to all men,
or we must see men die, and then die ourselves.

SELF-PROTECTION

When science starts to be interpretive
it is more unscientific even than mysticism.

To make self-preservation and self-protection the first law of
    existence
is about as scientific as making suicide the first law of exist-
    ence,
and amounts to very much the same thing.

A nightingale singing at the top of his voice
is neither hiding himself nor preserving himself nor propagat-
    ing his species;
he is giving himself away in every sense of the word;
and obviously, it is the culminating point of his existence.

A tiger is striped and golden for his own glory.
He would certainly be much more invisible if he were grey-
    green.

And I don't suppose the ichthyosaurus sparkled like the
    humming-bird,
no doubt he was khaki-coloured with muddy protective
    coloration,
so why didn't he survive?

As a matter of fact, the only creatures that seem to survive
are those that give themselves away in flash and sparkle
and gay flicker of joyful life;
those that go glittering abroad
with a bit of splendour.

Even mice play quite beautifully at shadows,
and some of them are brilliantly piebald.

I expect the dodo looked like a clod,
a drab and dingy bird.

A MAN

ALL I care about in a man
is that unbroken spark in him
where he is himself
undauntedly.

And all I want is to see the spark flicker
vivid and clean.

But our civilisation, alas,
with lust crushes out the spark
and leaves men living clay.

Because when the spark is crushed in a man
he can't help being a slave, a wage-slave,
a money-slave.

LIZARD

A LIZARD ran out on a rock and looked up, listening
no doubt to the sounding of the spheres.
And what a dandy fellow! the right toss of a chin for you
and swirl of a tail!

If men were as much men as lizards are lizards
they'd be worth looking at.

RELATIVITY

I LIKE relativity and quantum theories
because I don't understand them
and they make me feel as if space shifted about like a swan
    that can't settle,
refusing to sit still and be measured;
and as if the atom were an impulsive thing
always changing its mind.

SPACE

Space, of course, is alive
that's why it moves about;
and that's what makes it eternally spacious and unstuffy.

And somewhere it has a wild heart
that sends pulses even through me;
and I call it the sun;
and I feel aristocratic, noble, when I feel a pulse go through me
from the wild heart of space, that I call the sun of suns.

SUN-MEN

Men should group themselves into a new order
of sun-men.
Each one turning his breast straight to the sun of suns
in the centre of all things,
and from his own little inward sun
nodding to the great one.

And receiving from the great one
his strength and his promptings,
and refusing the pettifogging promptings of human weakness.

And walking each in his own sun-glory
with bright legs and uncringing buttocks.

SUN-WOMEN

How strange it would be if some women came forward and said:
We are sun-women!
We belong neither to men nor our children nor even ourselves
but to the sun.

And how delicious it is to feel sunshine upon one!
And how delicious to open like a marigold
when a man comes looking down upon one
with sun in his face, so that a woman cannot but open
like a marigold to the sun,
and thrill with glittering rays.

DEMOCRACY

I AM a democrat in so far as I love the free sun in men
and an aristocrat in so far as I detest narrow-gutted, possessive persons.

I love the sun in any man
when I see it between his brows
clear, and fearless, even if tiny.

But when I see these grey successful men
so hideous and corpse-like, utterly sunless,
like gross successful slaves mechanically waddling,
then I am more than radical, I want to work a guillotine.

And when I see working men
pale and mean and insect-like, scuttling along
and living like lice, on poor money
and never looking up,
then I wish, like Tiberius, the multitude had only one head
so that I could lop it off.

I feel that when people have gone utterly sunless
they shouldn't exist.

ARISTOCRACY OF THE SUN

To be an aristocrat of the sun
you don't need one single social inferior to exalt you;
you draw your nobility direct from the sun
let other people be what they may.

I am that I am
from the sun,
and people are not my measure.

Perhaps, if we started right, all the children could grow up sunny
and sun-aristocrats.
We need have no dead people, money-slaves, and social worms.

CONSCIENCE

CONSCIENCE
is sun-awareness
and our deep instinct
not to go against the sun.

THE MIDDLE CLASSES

THE middle classes
are sunless.
They have only two measures:
mankind and money,
they have utterly no reference to the sun.

As soon as you let *people* be your measure
you are middle-class and essentially non-existent.

Because, if the middle classes had no poorer people to be
    superior to
they would themselves at once collapse into nullity.
And if they had no upper classes either, to be inferior to,
they wouldn't suddenly become themselves aristocratic,
they'd become nothing.
For their middleness is only an unreality separating two realities.

No sun, no earth,
nothing that transcends the bourgeois middlingness,
the middle classes are more meaningless
than paper money when the bank is broke.

IMMORALITY

It is only immoral
to be dead-alive,
sun-extinct
and busy putting out the sun
in other people.

CENSORS

Censors are dead men
set up to judge between life and death.
For no live, sunny man would be a censor,
he'd just laugh.

But censors, being dead men,
have a stern eye on life.
—That thing's alive! It's dangerous. Make away with it!—
And when the execution is performed
you hear the stertorous, self-righteous heavy breathing of the
    dead men,
the censors, breathing with relief.

MAN'S IMAGE

What a pity, when a man looks at himself in a glass
he doesn't bark at himself, like a dog does,
or fluff up in indignant fury, like a cat!

What a pity he sees himself so wonderful,
a little lower than the angels!
and so interesting!

IMMORAL MAN

Man is immoral because he has got a mind
and can't get used to the fact.

The deep instincts, when left alone, are quite moral,
and clear intuition is more than moral,
it really makes us men.

Why don't we learn to tame the mind
instead of killing the passions and the instincts and feelings?
It is the mind which is uncouth and overweening
and ruins our complex harmony.

COWARDS

In all creation, only man cowers and is afraid of life.
Only man is terrified of his own possible splendour and delight.
Only is man agonised in front of the necessity to be something
    better than he is,
poor mental worm.

Though maybe the mammoth got too big in tusk and teeth,
and the extinct giant elk too big in antlers,
out of fear of the unknown enemy;
so perhaps they too died out from fear,
as man is likely to do.

THINK——!

IMAGINE what it must have been to have existence
in the wild days when life was sliding whirlwinds, blue-hot weights,
in the days called chaos, which left us rocks, and gems!

Think that the sapphire is only alumina, like kitchen pans
crushed utterly, and breathed through and through
with fiery weight and wild life, and coming out
clear and flowery blue!

PEACOCK

THINK how a peacock in a forest of high trees
shimmers in a stream of blueness and long-tressed magnificence!
And women even cut their shimmery hair!

PALTRY-LOOKING PEOPLE

AND think how the nightingale, who is so shy,
makes of himself a belfry of throbbing sound!
While people mince mean words through their teeth.

And think how wild animals trot with splendour
till man destroys them!
how vividly they make their assertion of life!

But how paltry, mingy and dingy and squalid people look
in their rag garments scuttling through the streets,
or sitting stuck like automata in automobiles!

TARTS

I suppose tarts are called tarts because they're tart,
meaning sour, make you pull a face after.
And I suppose most girls are a bit tarty to-day,
so that's why so many young men have long faces.
The father eats the pear, and the son's teeth are set on edge.

LATTER-DAY SINNERS

The worst of the younger generation, those Latter-Day sinners,
is that they calmly assert: We only thrill to perversity,
    murder, suicide, rape—
bragging a little, really,
and at the same time, expect to go on calmly eating good
    dinners for the next fifty years.

They say: *Après moi le déluge!* and calmly expect
that the deluge will never be turned on them, only *after* them.

Post me, nihil!—But perhaps, my dears,
nihil will come along and hit you on the head.

Why should the deluge wait while these young gentry go on
    eating
good dinners for fifty more long years?
Why should our Latter-Day sinners expect such a long smooth
    run
for their very paltry little bit of money?

If you are expecting a Second Advent in the shape of a deluge
you mustn't expect it also to wait for your convenience.

FATE AND THE YOUNGER GENERATION

IT is strange to think of the Annas, the Vronskys, the Pierres,
    all the Tolstoyan lot
wiped out.

And the Alyoshas and Dmitris and Myshkins and Stavrogins,
    the Dostoevsky lot
all wiped out.

And the Tchekov wimbly-wambly wet-legs all wiped out.

Gone! Dead, or wandering in exile with their feathers plucked,
anyhow, gone from what they were, entirely.

Will the Proustian lot go next?
And then our English imitation intelligentsia?
Is it the *Quos vult perdere Deus* business?

Anyhow the Tolstoyan lot simply asked for extinction:
Eat me up, dear peasant!—So the peasant ate him.
And the Dostoevsky lot wallowed in the thought:
Let me sin my way to Jesus!—So they sinned themselves off
    the face of the earth.
And the Tchekov lot: I'm too weak and lovable to live!—So
    they went.
Now the Proustian lot: Dear darling death, let me wriggle my
    way towards you

like the worm I am!—So he wriggled and got there.
Finally our little lot: I don't want to die, but by Jingo if I
    do!—
—Well, it won't matter so very much, either.

AS FOR ME, I'M A PATRIOT

Whatever else they say of me
they'll never be able to say
I was one of the little blighters
who so brilliantly betray
the tough old England that made us
and in them is rotting away.

I'd betray the middle classes
and money and industry
and the intellectual asses
and cash christianity,

but not the England that made me
the stuff of a man,
the old England that doesn't upbraid me,
nor put me under a ban.

THE ROSE OF ENGLAND

Oh the rose of England is a single rose
and damasked red and white!

But roses, if they're fed too much,
change from being single and become gradually double,
and that's what's happened to the English rose.

The wild rose in a sheltered garden
when it need struggle no more
softly blows out its thin little male stamens
into broad sweet petals,
and through the centuries goes on and on
puffing its little male stamens out into sterile petal flames
till at last it's a full, full rose, and has no male dust any more
it propagates no more.

So it is with Englishmen.
They are all double roses
and their true maleness is gone.

Oh the rose of England is a single rose
and needs to be raised from seed.

ENGLAND IN 1929

ENGLAND was always a country of men
and had a brave destiny, even when she went wrong.

Now it's a country of frightened old mongrels
snapping out of fear,
and young wash-outs pretending to be in love with death
yet living on the fat of the land;

so of course the nation is swollen with insoluble problems
and like to become incurably diseased inside.

LIBERTY'S OLD OLD STORY

MEN fight for liberty, and win it with hard knocks.
Their children, brought up easy, let it slip away again, poor
    fools.
And their grandchildren are once more slaves.

NEW BROOMS

NEW brooms sweep clean
but they often raise such a dust in the sweeping
that they choke the sweeper.

POLICE SPIES

START a system of official spying
and you've introduced anarchy into your country

NOW IT'S HAPPENED

ONE cannot now help thinking
how much better it would have been
if Vronsky and Anna Karenin
had stood up for themselves, and seen
Russia across her crisis,
instead of leaving it to Lenin.

The big, flamboyant Russia
might have been saved, if a pair
of rebels like Anna and Vronsky
had blasted the sickly air
of Dostoevsky and Tchekov,
and spy-government everywhere.

But Tolstoi was a traitor
to the Russia that needed him most,
the clumsy, bewildered Russia
so worried by the Holy Ghost.
He shifted his job on to the peasants
and landed them all on toast.

Dostoevsky, the Judas,
with his sham christianity
epileptically ruined
the last bit of sanity
left in the hefty bodies
of the Russian nobility.

So our goody-good men betray us
and our sainty-saints let us down,
and a sickly people will slay us
if we touch the sob-stuff crown
of such martyrs; while Marxian tenets
naturally take hold of the town.

Too much of the humble Willy wet-leg
and the holy can't-help-it touch,
till you've ruined a nation's fibre
and they loathe all feeling as such,
and want to be cold and devilish hard
like machines—and you can't wonder much.—

ENERGETIC WOMEN

Why are women so energetic?
prancing their knees under their tiny skirts
like war-horses; or war-ponies at least!

Why are they so centrifugal?
Why are they so bursting, flinging themselves about?
Why, as they grow older, do they suffer from blood-pressure?

Why are they never happy to be still?
Why did they cut off their long hair
which they could comb by the hour in luxurious quiet?

I suppose when the men all started being Willy wet-legs
women felt it was no longer any use being a linger-longer-Lucy

FILM PASSION

IF all those females who so passionately loved
the film face of Rudolf Valentino
had had to take him for one night only, in the flesh,
how they'd have hated him!

Hated him just because he was a man
and flesh of a man.
For the luscious filmy imagination loathes the male substance
with deadly loathing.

All the women who adored the shadow of the man on the
    screen
helped to kill him in the flesh.
Such adoration pierces the loins and perishes the man
worse than the evil eye.

FEMALE COERCION

IF men only fought outwards into the world
women might be devoted and gentle.
The fight's got to go in some direction.

But when men turn Willy wet-legs
women start in to make changes;
only instead of changing things that might be changed
they want to change the man himself
and turn the poor silk glove into a lusty sow's ear.

And the poor Willy wet-legs, the soft silk gloves,
how they hate the women's efforts to turn them
into sow's ears!

The modern Circe-dom!

VOLCANIC VENUS

What has happened in the world?
the women are like little volcanoes
all more or less in eruption.

It is very unnerving, moving in a world of smouldering volcanoes.
It is rather agitating, sleeping with a little Vesuvius.
And exhausting, penetrating the lava-crater of a tiny Ixtaccihuatl
and never knowing when you'll provoke an earthquake.

WONDERFUL SPIRITUAL WOMEN

The wonderful thoughtful women who make such good companions to a man
are only sitting tight on the craters of their volcano
and spreading their skirts.

Or like the woman who sat down on a sleeping mastodon
thinking he was a little hill, and she murmured such beautiful things
the men stood around like crocuses agape in the sun.

Then suddenly the mastodon rose with the wonderful lady
and trampled all the listeners to a smush.

POOR BIT OF A WENCH!——

WILL no one say hush! to thee,
poor lass, poor bit of a wench?
Will never a man say: Come, my pigeon,
come an' be still wi' me, my own bit of a wench!

And would you peck out his eyes if he did?

WHAT AILS THEE?——

WHAT ails thee then, woman, what ails thee?
doesn't ter know?

If tha canna say't, come then an' scraight it out on my bosom
Eh?—Men doesna ha'e bosoms? 'appen not, on'y tha knows
    what I mean.
Come then, tha can scraight it out on my shirt-front
an' tha'lt feel better.

> — In the first place, I don't scraight.
> And if I did, I certainly couldn't *scraight it out*.
> And if I could, the last place I should choose
> would be your shirt-front
> or your manly bosom either.
> So leave off trying to put the Robbie Burns touch
>   over me
> and kindly hand me the cigarettes
> if you haven't smoked them all,
> which you're much more likely to do
> than to shelter anybody from the cau-auld blast.——

IT'S NO GOOD!

It's no good, the women are in eruption,
and those that have been good so far
now begin to steam ominously,
and if they're over forty-five, hurl great stones into the air
which are very like to hit you on the head as you sit
on the very slopes of the matrimonial mountain
where you've sat peacefully all these years.

Vengeance is mine, saith the Lord,
but the women are my favourite vessels of wrath.

SHIPS IN BOTTLES

O SHIP in a bottle
with masts erect and spars all set and sails spread
how you remind me of my London friends,
O ships in bottles!

Little fleets
that put to sea on certain evenings,
frigates, barks and pinnaces, yawls
all beautifully rigged and bottled up
that put to sea and boldly sink Armadas
in a pub parlour, in literary London, on certain evenings.

O small flotilla of sorry souls
sail on, over perilous seas of thought,
cast your little anchors in ports of eternity,
then weigh, and out to the infinities,
skirting the poles of being and of not-being.

Ah, in that parlour of the London pub
what dangers, ah what dangers!
Caught between great icebergs of doubt
they are all but crushed
little ships.
Nipped upon the frozen floods of philosophic despair
they lie high and dry,
high and dry.
Reeling in the black end of all beliefs
they sink.

Yet there they are, there they are,
little ships
safe inside their bottles!

Whelmed in profundities of profound conversation,
lost between great waves of ultimate ideas
they are—why there they are,
safe inside their bottles!

Safer than in the arms of Jesus!
Oh safer than anything else is a well-corked, glassy ego,
and sounder than all insurance is a shiny mental conceit!

Sail, little ships in your glass bottles
safe from every contact,
safe from all experience,
safe, above all, from life!

And let the nodding tempests of verbosity
weekly or twice-weekly whistle round your bottles.
Spread your small sails immune, little ships!
The storm is words, the bottles never break.

KNOW THYSELF, AND THAT THOU ART MORTAL

If you want to know yourself
you've got to keep up with yourself.
Your self moves on, and is not to-day what it was yesterday;
and you've got to run, to keep up with it.

But sometimes we run ahead too fast
running after a figment of ourselves.
And that's what we've done to-day.

We think we're such clever little johnnies
with our sharp little eyes and our high-power machines
which get us ahead so much faster than our feet could ever
    carry us.

When alas, it's only part of our clever little self that gets
    ahead!
Something is left behind, lost and howling, and we know it.

Ah, clever Odysseus who outwitted the cylcop
and blinded him in his one big eye,
put out a light of consciousness and left a blinded brute.

Clever little ants in spectacles, we are,
performing our antics.

But what we also are, and we need to know it,
is blinded brutes of cyclops, with our cyclopean eye put out.

And we still bleed, and we grope and roar;
for spectacles and bulging clever ant-eyes are no good to the
    cyclop,
he wants his one great wondering eye, the eye of the cavern
    and the portent.

As little social ants perhaps we function all right.
But oh, our human lives, the lunging blind cyclops we are!
hitting ourselves against unseen rock, crashing our head against the roof
of the ancient cave, smashing into one another,
tearing each other's feelings, trampling each other's tenderest emotions to mud
and never knowing what we are doing, roaring blind with pain and dismay.

Ah, cyclops, the little ant-men can never enlighten you
with their bulging policeman's-lamp eyes.
You need your own great wondering eye that flashes with instinct in the cavern
and gleams on the world with the warm dark vision of intuition!

Even our brilliantest young intellectuals
are also poor blind cyclops, moaning
with all the hurt to their instinctive and emotional selves,
and grieving with puppy-like blind crying
over their mutilated cyclopean eye.

WHAT IS MAN WITHOUT AN INCOME?——

WHAT is man without an income?
—Well, let him get on the dole!

Dole, dole, dole
hole, hole, hole
soul, soul, soul—

What is man without an income?
Answer without a rigmarole.

On the dole, dole, dole
he's a hole, hole, hole
in the nation's pocket.

—Now then, you leave a man's misfortunes alone

He's got a soul, soul, soul
but the coal, coal, coal
on the whole, whole, whole
doesn't pay,
so the dole, dole, dole's
the only way.

And on the dole, dole, dole
a man's a hole, hole, hole
in the nation's pocket,
and his soul, soul, soul
won't stop a hole, hole, hole
though his ashes might.

Immortal Cæsar dead and turned to clay
would stop a hole to keep the wind away.

But a man without a job
isn't even as good as a gob
of clay.

Body and soul
he's just a hole
down which the nation's resources roll
away.

CANVASSING FOR THE ELECTION

— Excuse me, but are you a superior person?
— I beg your pardon?
— Oh, I'm sure you'll understand. We're making a census of all the *really* patriotic people—the right sort of people, you know—of course you understand what I mean—so *would* you mind giving me your word?—and signing here, please—that you *are* a superior person—that's all we need to know—
— Really, I don't know what you take me for!
— Yes, I know! It's too bad! Of course it's perfectly superfluous to ask, but the League insists. Thank you so much! No, sign here, please, and there I countersign. That's right! Yes, that's all!—*I declare I am a superior person*—. Yes, exactly! and here I countersign your declaration. It's so simple, and really, it's *all* we need to know about anybody. And do you know, I've never been denied a signature! We English *are* a solid people, after all. This proves it. Quite! Thank you so much! We're getting on simply splendidly—and it *is* a comfort, isn't it?—

ALTERCATION

Now look here,
if you were really superior,
really superior,
you'd have money, and you know it!

Well what abaht it?

What about it?
what about it?

why, isn't it obvious?
Here you are, with no money,
and here am I, paying income tax and god-knows-what taxes
just to support you and find you money,
and you stand there and expect me to treat you like an
    equal!—
Whereas, let me tell you, if you *were* my equal
you'd *have* money, you'd *have* it, enough to support yourself,
    anyhow—
And there you stand with *nothing*, and expect me to hand it
    you out
as if it were your dues, and I didn't count at all—

All right, guvnor! What abaht it?

Do you mean to say what about it?
My God, it takes some beating!
If you were a *man*, and up to my mark, you'd *have* money—
    can't you see it?
You're my inferior, that's what you are, you're my inferior.
And do you think it's my business to be handing out money
    to a lot of inferior swipe?
Eh? Answer me that!

Right ch'are, boss! An' what abaht it?

FINDING YOUR LEVEL

Down, down, down!
There must be a nadir somewhere
of superiority.

Down, and still
the superior persons, though somewhat inferior,
are still superior.

They are still superior, so there must be something they are
    superior to.
There must be a bed-rock somewhere, of people who are not
    superior,
one must come down to *terra firma* somewhere!

Or must one simply say:
All my inferiors are very superior.

There has been great progress
in superiority.

Fortunately though, some superior persons are still superior
to the quite superior persons who are not so superior as they
    are.

May I ask if you are *really* superior
or if you only look it so wonderfully?
Because we English *do* appreciate a *real* gentleman, or a *real*
    lady;
but appearances *are* deceptive nowadays, aren't they?

And if you only *look* so distinguished and superior
when really you are slightly inferior,
like a shop-lady or a lady-secretary,
you mustn't expect, my dear, to get away with it.
There's a list kept of the truly superior
and if you're not on the list, why there you are, my dear,
you're off it.

There are great numbers of quite superior persons who are
    not on the list,
poor things—but we can't help that, can we!
We must draw a line somewhere
or we should never know when we were crossing the equator.

What is man, that thou art mindful of him,
or the son of man, that thou pitiest him?
for thou hast made him a little lower than the angels
who are *very* superior people,
Oh *very!*

CLIMBING UP

WHEN you climb up to the middle classes
you leave a lot behind you,
you leave a lot, you've lost a lot
and you've nobody to remind you
of all the things they squeezed out of you
when they took you and refined you.

When they took you and refined you
they squeezed out most of your guts;
they took away your good old stones
and gave you a couple of nuts;
and they taught you to speak King's English
and butter your slippery buts.

Oh you've got to be like a monkey
if you climb up the tree!
You've no more use for the solid earth
and the lad you used to be.
You sit in the boughs and gibber
with superiority.

They all gibber and gibber and chatter,
and never a word they say
comes really out of their guts, lad,
they make it up half way;
they make it up, and it's always the same,
if it's serious or if it's play.

You think they're the same as you are
and then you find they're not,
and they never were nor would be,
not one of the whole job lot.
And you have to act up like they do
or they think you're off your dot.

There isn't a man among 'em,
not one; they all seemed to me
like monkeys or angels or something, in a limited
liability company;
like a limited liability company
they are, all limited liability.

What they're limited to or liable
to, I could never make out.
But they're all alike, an' it makes you
want to get up an' shout
an' blast 'em forever; but they'd only
think you a lower-class lout.

I tell you, something's been done to 'em,
to the pullets up above;
there's not a cock bird among 'em
though they're always on about love,
an' you could no more get 'em a move on,
no! no matter how you may shove!

CONUNDRUMS

TELL me a word
that you've often heard,
yet it makes you squint
if you see it in print!

Tell me a thing
that you've often seen,
yet if put in a book
it makes you turn green!

Tell me a thing
that you often do,
which described in a story
shocks you through and through!

Tell me what's wrong
with words or with you
that you don't mind the thing
yet the name is taboo.

A RISE IN THE WORLD——

I ROSE up in the world, Ooray!
rose very high, for me.
An earl once asked me down to stay
and a duchess once came to tea.

I didn't stay very long with the earl
and the duchess has done with me.
But still, I rose quite high in the world
don't you think?—or don't you agree?

But now I am slithering down again,
down the trunk of the slippery tree;
I find I'd rather get back to earth,
where I belong, you see.

Up there I didn't like it,
chattering, though not with glee,
the whole of the time, and nothing
mattering—at least, not to me.

God, let me get down to earth again
away from the upper ten
millions—for there's millions of 'em
up there—but not any men.

UP HE GOES!——

Up I rose, my lads, an' I heard yer
sayin': Up he goes!

Up like a bloomin' little Excelsior
in his Sunday clothes!

Up he goes, up the bloomin' ladder
about to the giddy top!
Who'd ever have thought it of that lad, a
pasty little snot!—

Never you mind, my lads, I left you
a long long way behind.
You'll none of you rise in the world like I did
an' if you did, you'd find

it damn well wasn't worth it,
goin' up an' bein' refined;
it was nowt but a dirty sell, that's all,
a *damn fraud*, underlined.

They're not any better than we are,
the upper classes—they're worse.
Such bloomin' fat-arsed dool-owls
they aren't even fit to curse!

There isn't a damn thing in 'em,
they're as empty as empty tins;
they haven't the spunk of a battle-twig
an' all they can think of is sins.

No, there's nowt in the upper classes
as far as I can find;
a worse lot o' jujubey asses
than the lot I left behind.

They'll never do a thing, boys,
they can't, they're simply fused.
So if any of you's live wires, with wits
to use, they'd better be used.

If there's anything got to be done, why
get up an' do it yourselves!
Though God knows if you're any better
sittin' there in rows on your shelves!

An' if you're not any better,
if you've none of you got more spunk
than they've got in the upper classes,
why, let's all of us do a bunk.

We're not fit for the earth we live on,
we're not fit for the air we breathe.
We'd better get out, an' make way for
the babes just beginning to teethe.

THE SADDEST DAY

" We climbed the steep ascent to heaven
    Through peril, toil and pain.
  O God to us may strength be given
    To scramble back again."

O I was born low and inferior
but shining up beyond
I saw the whole superior
world shine like the promised land.

So up I started climbing
to join the folks on high,
but when at last I got there
I had to sit down and cry.

For it wasn't a bit superior,
it was only affected and mean;
though the house had a fine interior
the people were never in.

I mean, they were never entirely
there when you talked to them;
away in some private cupboard
some small voice went: *Ahem!*

Ahem! they went. *This fellow
is a little too open for me;
with such people one has to be careful
though, of course, we won't let him see!—*

And they thought you couldn't hear them
privately coughing: *Ahem!*
And they thought you couldn't see them
cautiously swallowing their phlegm!

But of course I always heard them,
and every time the same.
They all of them always kept up their sleeve
their class-superior claim.

Some narrow-gutted superiority,
and trying to make you agree,
which, for myself, I couldn't,
it was all my-eye to me.

And so there came the saddest day
when I had to tell myself plain:
the upper classes are just a fraud,
you'd better get down again.

PRESTIGE

I never met a single
middle-class person whose
nerves didn't tighten against me
as if they'd got something to lose.

Though what it was, you can ask me:
some mysterious sort of prestige
that was nothing to me; though they always
seemed to think I was laying it siege.

It was something I never could fathom,
that mysterious prestige which they all
seemed to think they'd got, like a halo
around them, an invisible wall.

If *you* were willing to see it
they were only too eager to grant
you a similar glory, since you'd risen
to their levels, my holy aunt!

But never, no never could I see it,
and so I could never feel
the proper unction about it,
and it worried me a good deal.

For years and years it bothered me
that I couldn't feel one of them,
till at last I saw the reason:
they were just a bloody sham.

As far as any superiority
or halo or prestige went
they were just a bloody collective fraud,
that was what their *Ahem!* meant.

Their superiority was meanness,
they were cunning about the goods
and sly with a lot of after-thought,
and they put it over us, the duds!

And I'd let myself be swindled
half believing 'em, till one day
I suddenly said: I've finished!
My God, let me get away!

HAVE DONE WITH IT

ONCE and for all, have done with it,
all the silly bunk
of upper-class superiority; that superior
stuff is just holy skunk.

Just you walk around them
and look at the fat-eyed lot
and tell me how they can put it across,
this superior rot!

All these gracious ladies
graciously bowing down
from their pedestals! Holy Moses
they've done you brown!

And all the sacred gentry
so responsible and good,
feeling so *kind* towards you
and suckin' your blood!

My! the bloomin' pompoms!
Even as trimmings they're stale.
Still, if you don't want to bother,
I don't care myself a whale.

HENRIETTE

O Henriette
I remember yet
how cross you were
over Lady C.
how you hated her
and detested me.

Yet now you see
you don't mind a bit.
You've got used to it,
and you feel more free.

And now you know
how good we were
up there in the snow
with Lady C.
though you hated her
at the first go.

Yet now you can see
how she set us free
to laugh, and to be
more spontaneous, and we
were happy, weren't we
up there in the snow
with the world below !

So now, when you say
your prayers at night
you must sometimes pray :

Dear Lord of delight
may I be Jane
to-night, profane
but sweet in your sight,
though last night I was Mary—

You said I might
dear Lord of right
be so contrary.
So may I be Jane
to-night, and refrain
from being Mary?—

VITALITY

Alas, my poor young men,
do you lack vitality?

Has the shell grown too heavy for the tortoise?
Does he just squirm?

Is the frame of things too heavy
for poor young wretched men?
Do they jazz and jump and wriggle
and rush about in machines
and listen to bodiless noises
and cling to their thin young women
as to the last straw

just in desperation,
because their spirit can't move?
Because their hope is pinned down by the system
and can't even flutter?

Well well, if it is so it is so;
but remember, the undaunted gods
give vitality still to the dauntless.

And sometimes they give it as love,
ah love, sweet love, not so easy!
But sometimes they give it as lightning.

And it's no good wailing for love
if they only offer you lightning.
And it's no good mooning for sloppy ease
when they're holding out the thunderbolt
for you to take.

You might as well take the lightning
for once, and feel it go through you.
You might as well accept the thunderbolt
and prepare for storms.

You'll not get vitality any other way.

WILLY WET-LEG

I can't stand Willy wet-leg,
can't stand him at any price.
He's resigned, and when you hit him
he let's you hit him twice.

MAYBE——

Ah well! ah well! maybe
the young have learned some sense.
They ought at last to see through the game
they've sat long enough on the fence.

Maybe their little bottoms
will get tired and sore at last
of sitting there on the fence, and letting
their good youth go to waste.

Maybe a sense of destiny
will rise in them one day,
maybe they'll realise it's time
they slipped into the fray.

Maybe they're getting tired
of sitting on the fence;
it dawns on them that the whole damn swindle
is played at their expense.

STAND UP!——

STAND up, but not for Jesus!
It's a little late for that.
Stand up for justice and a jolly life.
I'll hold your hat.

Stand up, stand up for justice,
ye swindled little blokes!
Stand up and do some punching,
give 'em a few hard pokes.

Stand up for jolly justice
you haven't got much to lose:
a job you don't like and a scanty chance
for a dreary little booze.

Stand up for something different,
and have a little fun
fighting for something worth fighting for
before you've done.

Stand up for a new arrangement
for a chance of life all round,
for freedom, and the fun of living
bust in, and hold the ground!

TRUST

OH we've got to trust
one another again
in some essentials.

Not the narrow little
bargaining trust
that says: I'm for you
if you'll be for me.—

But a bigger trust,
a trust of the sun
that does not bother
about moth and rust,
and we see it shining
in one another.

Oh don't you trust me,
don't burden me
with your life and affairs; don't thrust me
into your cares.

But I think you may trust
the sun in me
that glows with just
as much glow as you see
in me, and no more.

But if it warms
your heart's quick core
why then trust it, it forms
one faithfulness more.

And be, oh be
a sun to me,
not a weary, insistent
personality

but a sun that shines
and goes dark, but shines
again and entwines
with the sunshine in me

till we both of us
are more glorious
and more sunny.

www.ingramcontent.com/pod-product-compliance
Lightning Source LLC
Chambersburg PA
CBHW011615170426
43195CB00042B/2888